Management Would Be Easy...
If It Weren't for the People

Management Would Be Easy...
If It Weren't for the People

Patricia J. Addesso, Ph.D.

American Management Association

New York · Atlanta · Boston · Chicago · Kansas City · San Francisco · Washington, D.C.
Brussels · Mexico City · Tokyo · Toronto

This publication is designed to provide accurate and authoritative
information in regard to the subject matter covered. It is sold with the
understanding that the publisher is not engaged in rendering legal,
accounting, or other professional service. If legal advice or other expert
assistance is required, the services of a competent professional person
should be sought.

Library of Congress Cataloging-in-Publication Data

Addesso, Patricia J.
        Management would be easy— if it weren't for the people / Patricia
J. Addesso.
        p.   cm.
    Includes bibliographical references and index.
    ISBN 0-8144-7915-4
    1. Personnel management. 2. Psychology, Industrial.   I. Title.
HF5549.A46   1996
158.7—dc20   96–19541
                                                                  CIP

Printing number

10   9   8   7   6   5   4   3

Contents

Introduction

If you are a manager, an executive, a supervisor, or a team leader, your job requires that you influence other people's behavior. Many of us find this a challenging and frustrating task. Managers write policies, give out rewards, and issue orders, only to find that sometimes employees still don't do what they're supposed to do. To manage people more effectively, we need to broaden our view of what it means to exert influence. Efforts to *influence* behavior can be more effective if managers concentrate first on *understanding* the behavior.

Management is an art, and it requires a delicate balance between technical skills and people skills. While organizations do a fairly good job preparing people for the technical aspects of their jobs, frustration often arises when a technically skilled individual is asked to manage other people, which calls for an entirely new and different set of skills and knowledge.

Who gets promoted in organizations? It is often the people who are best at what they do. The best teachers, for example, become principals. The best accountants become accounting department managers. Unfortunately, it is often assumed that management ability is somehow picked up through osmosis, that on-the-job training or a few seminars can teach people what they need to know to be effective managers. If these new managers ever took a course in human behavior, it is likely to have been

Psychology 101, in their first year in college. Some of them may have the ability to manage people; we call them the "born leaders." What if you are not a born leader? What if you need to find out more about what makes people tick?

In this book, you will find the concepts you learned about in Psychology 101 translated in a way that makes them of value to practicing managers. It has long been recognized that the basic truths about human behavior can be applied to the workplace. In fact, there is a whole field of endeavor, called industrial/organizational psychology, that does just that. The problem is that managers, executives, supervisors, and team leaders are not psychologists (and, in most cases, have no desire to be!). Even industrial psychology tends to be more a study of specific workplace applications, such as personnel selection and job design, than the study of basic psychological concepts as they apply to management. This book is for the manager who wants to manage people more effectively, managers who should not and cannot act as psychologists to the people who work for them. It is based on the premise that when organizations do not manage people well, it is often because their policies and procedures fly in the face of well-established psychological knowledge.

Those who work in organizations in the late twentieth century still struggle with the legacy of the Industrial Revolution. We work in organizations that are designed and run from a very mechanistic viewpoint and wonder why people are so much harder to manage than machines. Well-designed, well-built, well-maintained machines simply require new parts now and then. Even the computer age has led us to believe that as long as we get the command right, the machine will respond with just what we want it to do. Given these beliefs, it is not surprising that we experience a great deal of frustration as we try to manage people.

We know some things about people, thanks to many years of research in the behavioral sciences. We know about personality development, learning and behavior, perceptions, motivation, and other factors that drive behavior. What we have not always done is use this knowledge as we design organizational policy, structure, training, and jobs. Behavior is not a mystery. It usually has an identifiable cause and an identifiable goal. If you can influence the causes or the consequences of a behavior, you can change the behavior itself. Some organizations have gotten into trouble by not thinking through the implications of a policy or procedure and finding out too late that the undesirable results were predictable and logical.

Managing people effectively requires a longer-term perspective than managing technological issues. If you were to boot up a new piece of software, only to have your screen freeze, for example, you might get your internal software support person or an external help desk on the phone. You would describe what you see on the screen, and the support person would suggest a few possible causes for the problem and ask you to try a few things to fix it. The process for resolving people problems is similar and not at all mysterious. You might call me to describe some interpersonal problems that you observed at a staff meeting that morning. I could speculate as to a couple of possible causes (or maybe wish to observe it myself) and give you a couple of things to try to improve the situation. It just takes longer than a couple of keystrokes at your computer. When I hear things like "She should just grow up" or "They should just all get along," I think, "Yes, and your software should boot up perfectly each time. If it doesn't, you seek technical help. You don't berate the computer and tell it to grow up!"

In this book you will find a variety of simple psychological concepts applied to organizations. No book will give you all the answers to managing people, and you ought to be suspicious of any book that makes that claim. What this book will do is change your perspective on what it means to manage people and show you why it is a difficult, demanding, and sometimes frustrating business.

Each chapter concentrates on one of the basic bodies of knowledge about human behavior and opens with an organizational example that demonstrates how the concepts apply in the organizational world. Each chapter ends with a look back at the opening example to apply the concepts described in the chapter and a practical checklist of ideas that will help you remember the most important points. Throughout, the approach is practical, realistic, and down to earth.

If you are an engineer or a scientist or if you belong to some other discipline that requires a great deal of black-and-white, linear thinking, you may find a lot of the research in the behavioral sciences ambiguous. There are usually no clear-cut answers to people issues. If there were, management would be a science, not an art. More often than not, behavioral science research on a particular topic uses words such as "maybe," "sometimes," and "most" and phrases like "but" and "on the other hand." There are just too many individual differences among people to allow for universal truths. But don't let the absence of universal truths stop you from trying to be the best manager you can be. The real lesson here is that the most effective manager is the one who is able to adapt to a given situation or set of circumstances. Foster in yourself a flexibility and an adaptability, and begin by keeping an open mind to the fascinating truths about the people who work for you that you will find in the chapters that follow.

1

"I Gotta Be Me!" —*Personality*

Every person has a characteristic way of thinking, feeling, and behaving. The pattern is fairly consistent within the person and distinctive from one person to the next. We refer casually to people's personalities all the time, but why should a manager be concerned about the study of personality?

One of the defining characteristics of management jobs is that they involve influencing other people's behavior. Managers get things done through other people. Knowing about personality in general and giving some thought to the various personalities that report to you may help you explain your subordinates' behavior. Any greater understanding may also help you predict, and thus influence, that behavior.

Understanding personality leads to understanding behavior (Chapter 2), which is closely tied to motivation (Chapter 4). Although all of these topics are addressed separately, keep in mind that they are all linked and that an understanding of personality may help you better to motivate people and also lead to a more productive workplace.

The Thinkers vs. the Doers: Part 1

Mike's staff meetings have become ordeals for everyone concerned. The five managers who report to him are all bright, likable, capable people. Yet the meetings lately have turned into tense confrontations between two opposing camps.

Mike believes in participative management, and he expects his staff to reach decisions by arriving at a consensus. The problem is that Karen and Greg make up their minds very quickly and want to move on to the next agenda item. George wants more discussion, more data, and more time to think. Roger and Maria are not as vocal as George, but they back him up.

Mike is struggling to balance these two groups. Greg and Karen do seem to shoot from the hip sometimes, without thinking through all of the ramifications of the decision. George, on the other hand, does seem to be a foot-dragger and tends to mire the group in endless analysis. Mike has a hard time deciding which group to support, because both of them have made many high-quality decisions. Neither position seems to be "right."

Differences in the amount of time and data we need to be comfortable in making a decision are indicative of the numerous ways in which we differ from each other as our personalities develop. In this chapter, we will explore those differences and begin to see what a manager can do to handle personality conflicts.

How Does Personality Develop?

The two most influential schools of thought about personality development are the psychoanalytic and the humanistic views.

The name Sigmund Freud is inextricably linked to the psychoanalytic theories. According to Freud, events in our childhoods determine our personalities, and by age 5 or 6 our personalities are pretty well fixed. Our behavior is motivated by unconscious instincts, or drives, and we can trace most of our problems to unconscious thoughts, conflicts, and feelings that stem from repressed traumas in our childhood.

What does a manager need to know about Freud? Freudian theory explained a great deal about psychological problems in a way that was innovative and influential. When we talk about behavior at work, however, we're generally not talking about psychological problems. You are not equipped to deal with those and should not be expected to. Use (or get) an Employee Assistance Program (EAP), and make sure that people who have responsibility for other people (manager, supervisors, team leaders) are given training in how to make an EAP referral.

When we apply Freudian concepts to normal people, there are some things that a manager may find useful—the concept of defense mechanisms, for example. According to Freud, we all have unconscious drives and impulses that would make us feel very guilty and anxious if they were conscious. As our personalities develop, we become very good at things like repression, rationalization, projection, denial, and displacement. Although Freud talked about many defense mechanisms, understanding these five holds the most value for managing people in the workplace.

1. *Repression* refers to the process by which we muster our first line of defense. If a threatening or embarrassing thought attempts to intrude itself on our conscious mind, we push it out of conscious awareness. If we fail to repress the thought, one of the other defense mechanisms kicks in.

2. *Rationalization* is the process of coming up with logical or rational reasons to explain why we did some-

thing. We may have lied on our résumé, sabotaged a co-worker's career, or taken some other action that we felt was embarrassing or unacceptable. Before we even consciously admit it, the anxiety we feel causes us to invent socially acceptable reasons for the behavior ("Everyone lies on résumés. If I didn't, I would be putting myself at an unfair disadvantage.").

3. *Projection* involves "projecting" our unacceptable or embarrassing thoughts onto others around us. You may have seen this at work if you have ever had an employee approach you and confide that the rest of the department seemed to be thinking or feeling a certain way. The employee may seem to have a very nonjudgmental, "for the good of the department" attitude. For example, an employee may let you know that although he personally has no problem with it, the others in the group are concerned that the annual bonus will be smaller than they had expected. The employee may actually be quite incensed at the small bonus but unconsciously believes that he is above such petty bickering. He "projects" his feelings onto those around him.

4. When someone is engaged in *denial*, she simply ignores the reality of the situation. She may deny the existence of an unacceptable feeling or thought or the reality of an action she took. Although this behavior looks very odd to the outside observer, it does serve a purpose for the individual. When someone is clearly angry but denies it, it may be that she is uncomfortable with anger and prefers to ignore the existence of such an unpleasant feeling.

5. *Displacement* refers to the transfer of unacceptable feelings from the original target to a safer outlet. If your boss or a valuable customer treats you in a way that arouses a lot of anger and hostility in you, you have probably learned that it is not acceptable to act in a hostile manner in return. You may, however, transfer the

anger to your employees, your secretary, a peer, or your family in order to vent your pent-up feelings.

We all have our favorite defense mechanisms, and because they work for us, we have gotten pretty good at them. In fact, our preferred pattern of defense mechanisms is part of our personality. We are not doing these things consciously or in an attempt to fool other people; we are doing them to keep anxiety-producing thoughts and feelings from ourselves. Remember that you and the employees who work for you use defense mechanisms. They are unconscious and serve to reduce anxiety. It is self-defeating to attempt to point out someone's defenses and expect the person to thank you for your honesty. Don't delve too deeply into others' motivations, but simply point out to them the unacceptable nature of their behavior and suggest some alternatives. It is a lofty goal to hope to get someone to admit the real reason behind his behavior; according to Freud, none of us are capable of making such admissions on a regular basis. If we were, the anxiety would be too much to deal with.

In contrast to the somewhat pessimistic, dark view of mankind espoused by Freud and his followers, the humanistic school of personality development takes a much more uplifting view of human nature. According to humanistic psychologists (of whom Carl Rogers is perhaps the best known), development is a process that takes place as we strive to achieve our potential. Our inner drives, instead of being repressed childhood trauma, are the result of our innate desire for personal growth and higher levels of functioning. Rogers and his fellow psychologist Abraham Maslow have a great deal to offer today's practicing manager; the heart of their message involves the importance of self-esteem to our lives and our work.

Management seminars, workshops, and communication skills classes frequently exhort managers to maintain or enhance people's self-esteem. Whether you are reprimanding workers, praising them, or assigning tasks, you are advised to allow them to "save face," or maintain self-esteem.

Why? Is it just to be nice and create a warm and fuzzy workplace? No. There is abundant evidence that people who feel good about themselves perform better. High self-esteem is a win-win for the company and for the employee, but efforts to teach this concept to managers often fall on deaf ears. Managers listen and nod in a workshop, then quickly forget, in the press of business concerns, all that had sounded so logical in class.

People with high self-esteem accept bigger challenges. They react to failure by redoubling their efforts. People with low self-esteem expect to do poorly and often find their expectations met. With which type of person would you prefer to surround yourself? The defense mechanisms used by these people differ as well. A person with high self-esteem takes credit for positive outcomes, while ignoring or diminishing the importance of negative outcomes. The individual with low self-esteem, on the other hand, helps ensure the negative outcome that they are sure is going to happen anyway! In fact, they may consciously or unconsciously sabotage their own efforts so that when they fail, they can blame it on something else. Suppose an employee with low self-esteem is scheduled to give an important presentation to the board of directors on Monday morning. She might pick a fight with her family on Sunday, then stay up all night drinking beer so that when the presentation doesn't go well she has an external explanation for it.

What Kinds of Observable Behaviors Result From Personality?

The school of thought called behaviorism tells us that we don't really need to be concerned with inner drives, positive or negative. The human mind is essentially a "black box," and we can do no more than speculate about inner motivations. Behaviorists are far more concerned with the outer ramifications of personality, that is, behavior.

In Chapter 2, we are going to talk about learning and about the classical and operant conditioning approaches to thinking about learning. In general, behaviorists feel that personality does not explain behavior; learning does. Obviously, behaviorism has a great deal to offer managers, who make a living influencing other people's behavior. However, there is some value to understanding the behaviorist slant on personality theory. In this section we focus on behaviorism's contribution to the theory of personality, best described by the work of Albert Bandura.

Bandura felt that a concept called social learning provided a good explanation for most behavior. Behaviorists feel that reinforcement explains a lot of behavior, reinforcement being a reward that follows a behavior and increases the likelihood that the behavior will be repeated. Bandura said that observation also plays a part, that after we watch someone being rewarded for a behavior, we can model our behavior on that person's. He explained behavior as the result of *reciprocal determinism*, in which personality, the situation, and the consequences of behavior interact constantly. Obviously, just knowing someone's personality traits is of little value if you believe in reciprocal interaction.

In the earlier example of the employee who sabotaged her own presentation, the personality factors included pessimism and low self-esteem. The situation was a stressful one, and the consequences were not good (the presentation did not go well). A simple reading of behaviorism might cause us to think that because her behavior was not rewarded, the next time she had a presentation to make, she would do things differently.

Actually, though, the consequences were rewarding. We like to have our preconceived notions validated, and her beliefs about herself ("I can't do it") were supported by the outcome of the presentation. In an odd kind of way, this validation is rewarding to the individual with low self-esteem.

What Are the Components of Personality?

Personality theorists have focused a great deal of attention on *traits*. The general theories of personality focused on personality development, and, although they were interesting, they did not provide a practical framework for studying personality. Trait theorists concerned themselves more with what causes people to differ and what causes a particular individual to act in a characteristic way over time and across a variety of situations. Traits are not measured or even observed directly but are inferred by looking at behavior.

While all of us have numerous personality traits (we may be seen as aggressive, sociable, witty, and moody), some traits clearly have more influence on our everyday behavior than others. Traits can be classified as cardinal (traits that have a general influence on our behavior at all times), central (traits that are often detectable in our behavior), or secondary (traits that come into play in particular situations but are not vital parts of our personality). The strength of a trait often determines its classification. If Jim is extremely aggressive, it may be a cardinal trait because it is a very distinctive part of his personality. If he is aggressive only at certain times (in traffic, for example), aggression would be more of a secondary trait in him.

Many researchers have identified hundreds of models of personality traits, but there is a fairly substantial consensus around the five traits that can most efficiently describe a person. These five have been supported by a great deal of research and, more important, show up across cultures. We will look at each of the so-called big five and discuss how they affect the workplace and the manager's job.

Extroversion and Introversion

Most of us are fairly good at making judgments about whether other people are introverts or extroverts. We experience people as either talkative or quiet. We may find them sociable, outgoing, and open, or they may be reticent loners. For this trait, as well as all the other general and specific personality types, the most important piece of learning for a manager is that both types have a lot to offer in the workplace.

There are more extroverts than introverts in the world, and few things lead to greater misunderstandings in the workplace. Extroverts think by talking, and much of what they say (in meetings, for example) involves thinking out loud. Introverts think by mulling things over and need time and solitude to do so. When called upon to give her opinion in a meeting, an introvert may not feel prepared to do so. "I'll need to think about that" is a legitimate introvert need, but it may be seen by extroverts as a wishy-washy response. Over time, extroverts may stigmatize introverts as "always dodging the issue," while introverts may see extroverts as "full of hot air." A more nonjudgmental way of looking at the situation, and something a manager can foster in her work group, is to recognize the difference as legitimate and real; the manager can then create an environment that allows extroverts to talk things out and introverts to think things through.

As with all traits, the lesson is this: Both ends of the spectrum have their strengths and their weaknesses. A team needs both ends represented and needs to value the strengths that each type brings.

Agreeableness

The second of the "big five" traits is agreeableness. People fall somewhere on a continuum from cooperative and good-natured to irritable and negative. You may be wondering about the strengths and weaknesses in this case. What's wrong with being agreeable? The obvious weakness with agreeableness carried to an extreme is that the person may be unable to stand up for herself or buck the tide of popular opinion. Too good-natured, too mild, too cooperative—this is as big a drawback as being too negative, uncooperative, or irritable.

We like to label people and their traits as good or bad, but it should be clear by now that it is never that easy. Adaptability and flexibility—the ability to change with the situation—can be more important than any trait.

Conscientiousness

This trait compares the responsible, fussy, persevering person to the careless, undependable, flexible person. Again, people on either end of the spectrum may cause difficulties in organizations. A person who is too conscientious may be a real barrier to rapid change and getting things done. A perfectionist may spend all of his time and energy planning, not doing. The careless person may be of more assistance to you when you have a project that needs to get done quickly—not perfectly, but quickly.

Suppose you are trying to decide which person on your staff should be given a particular task. Gail is a perfectionist, and Tom is a little careless. The last time you gave Gail a project, it was done perfectly, but it took far more time than was allotted. Tom can get things done quickly, but there are apt to be a few rough edges. You need to ask yourself what the requirements of the current project are. Is time or quality the more heavily weighted criteria? Both Gail and Tom can be very helpful to you, depending on the job requirements. You can, of course, decide that both time and quality are important and let them work on the project jointly. This can work, but you are probably already seeing the problems that may arise; they might very well drive each other crazy.

Neuroticism

This trait refers to emotional stability. At one end of the continuum we find the calm, composed, poised individual. At the other end is the nervous, anxious, and excitable person. Are there any benefits in being somewhat neurotic or in having employees who are? Probably less clearly than for the other traits, but there are times that a nervous, excitable person may bring needed energy to a project. The task of the manager is to allow for the appropriate release of the nervous energy. This may mean assigning tasks on the basis of the fit between the person's need for activity and the demands of the task. An employee with a lot of nervous energy may not do well with a task that requires concentrated desk time.

The calm, composed employee may be seen as not having the sense of urgency that the project or job demands. Be careful when you find yourself making those kinds of judgments on the basis of an individual's demeanor. You cannot judge his sense of urgency from his nervousness or composure. In some organizations, the nervous, stressed, neurotic person gets a lot of credit because he always appears to be working hard, while the calm person (who may be getting just as much done) is too low-key to look busy.

Openness to Experience

The trait referred to as openness to experience is also called culture or sophistication. The fact that this trait has three names and that researchers have not been able to agree on just what it should be called is the first clue that this is a complicated matter. At one end of the spectrum are people who are intellectual, artistically sensitive, polished, refined, and imaginative. Some adjectives that have been used to describe the other end of the continuum are artistically insensitive, unreflective, narrow, crude, boorish, simple, and direct.

There is a great deal of snobbery evident in these adjectives and certainly in the understanding and managing of these personality types in the workplace. Keep in mind that most of us fall somewhere in the mid-ranges of most of these continuums; it is the rare individual who is found on the extremes. But it is still true that the "openness" trait influences many of the interpersonal transactions in the workplace.

Let's start with you. You probably think of yourself as somewhat intellectual, right? How reflective are you, really? As you read the last few paragraphs, were you thinking something like "How interesting! I never thought much about how a neurotic, undependable, disagreeable person could be of value in my work group." That may indicate a certain degree of openness to new ideas. An open person is also more able to be self-reflective and to think about her own personality and the effect it has on other people.

The biggest stumbling block in management education and development is a lack of reflective ability on the part of participants. The higher your level in management, the more resounding your successes, the more lavish your rewards, the harder it will be for you to learn anything new. If your style has worked for you in the past, why change it? In fact, why even reflect on it, since that would be pointless (and, Freud would say, anxiety-producing)?

None of us likes to number ourselves among the narrow-minded. The fact is, however, that too many of us are. Defensive behavior in managers leads them to read the latest management books, attend the latest seminars, nod wisely, then change nothing once they get back to the workplace. We all have this tendency, and the biggest favor we can do ourselves, our employees, and our organizations is to develop the ability to reflect on our personality and behavior and their effect on those around us.

Personality Theory and Productive Workplaces

Trait research has proved to be somewhat disappointing. Evidence for consistency in any one person has been sought for in vain, in most cases. Even if researchers were able to identify a person as aggressive, her behavior from situation to situation (with her child, her boss, a coworker, a competitor) would vary considerably depending upon the situation. Remember Bandura's reciprocal determinism; personality traits and the situation interact constantly to produce behavior, and knowing traits alone is never going to be enough to allow us to predict behavior. So what kinds of things does personality theory offer as we strive for a more productive workplace?

Assessment

Assessment refers to the measuring or describing of various characteristics of people. In the workplace, the typical assessment tool is a paper-and-pencil questionnaire.

Personality assessment can be used to hire people, place them into appropriate jobs, or put together teams with a variety of characteristics. Before you use a personality assessment for any of these purposes, however, ask some questions about the method used. A lot of inference is involved in personality testing. Does the test involve self-reporting? Does it compensate for the fact that the person may be giving socially acceptable answers? Do the questions disguise their real purpose? Is the test reliable and valid (any test vendor should be able to provide data on these two things)?

A well-known and widely used instrument is the Myers-Briggs Type Inventory, which can be very helpful in the workplace. The MBTI places people along four continuums. The first continuum is the Introversion/Extroversion scale, which, as we discussed earlier, has a powerful impact on people's behavior at work. The second continuum is Sensing and Intuition, a scale that describes how a person gathers data. Some people prefer to gather information through what they can see, hear, or touch (the senses) and thus tend to be very concrete, detail-oriented thinkers; others prefer to be intuitive and see possibilities and are conceptual thinkers concerned with the big picture. The third scale is the Thinking and Feeling scale. Once an individual has gathered the data he needs, he may prefer to make a decision based on logic, rationality, and facts (Thinking), or he may prefer to rely on personal values or the feelings of the people involved (Feeling). The fourth continuum is that of Judging and Perceiving. Judgers tend to take a "case closed" attitude once a decision is made, while Perceivers remain open to new ideas.

The MBTI has proven very helpful in helping managers understand personality differences in work teams and in putting the differences into a nonjudgmental framework. When two people take opposite approaches to problem solving (a Sensor-Thinker and an Intuitive-Feeler), they are quite likely to find each other very annoying. The MBTI allows them to realize that they are just looking at the situation through different perspectives and that the best decision may be reached by creating a synergy between the two perspectives.

Locus of Control

The personality theorist Julian Rotter explained many of the differences between personalities by the concept of locus of control. People with an internal locus of control feel that they can influence the outcome of events through their own efforts. When they succeed (or fail) at a task, they attribute the outcome to their own efforts (or their own shortcomings). Conversely, a person with an external locus of control attributes the outcome of most events to fate or chance. The effect on behavior is obvious; if my efforts make very little difference, why make a tremendous effort? There is a certain self-fulfilling prophecy at work here, too. (We will talk more about the self-fulfilling prophecy in Chapter 3.)

Explanatory Style

Every person has a characteristic explanatory style. Simply put, we all tend to be either optimistic or pessimistic in our outlook. Although optimists and pessimists differ in how they explain positive events, it is the explanation of negative events that has the potential to do the most damage to mood and to satisfaction with job and life.

Suppose one of your employees makes a presentation that goes badly. An optimist tends to see failures or setbacks as temporary and specific to the particular situation. His explanation of the event may go something like this: "I didn't prepare as well as I should have for Monday's presentation. I didn't handle Lois's questions very well. Next time I will be able to foresee some of her objections and prepare for them." A pessimist, on the other hand, sees negative events as permanent and universal. Her spoken or unspoken thoughts may go as follows: "Boy, did I blow it. I can't seem to get anything right [event is universal]. I guess I'll give up the thought of ever getting a promotion at this company [setback is permanent]."

Self-Efficacy

The concept of self-efficacy is related to the concept of self-esteem. Self-efficacy refers to the degree of confidence we have in ourselves. It directly influences what we attempt to do. A high degree of self-efficacy helps an employee attempt challenging tasks. Conversely, a low degree of self-efficacy may cause an individual to refrain from even attempting a task or challenge.

A style of management that encourages employees to feel confidence in themselves creates a win-win situation. The company benefits, the manager's job is easier, and the employee feels good about the job. What can you do to encourage employees' confidence in themselves? As when one is raising a child or coaching an athletic team, the answer lies in encouragement, helping the individual to succeed, and gradually raising expectations that allow for success to happen. Do you do everything you can to bolster your employees' confidence in themselves? It is important to do so, not just because it's the nice thing to do but because it makes for a more productive workplace. If you come from a technical background, you may not be comfortable with the soft side of management, but aside from your discomfort, the techniques of encouragement are inexpensive and have tremendous payback. Give it a try.

Handling Conflict

One of the most important tools managers can take away from personality theory is the help it gives in handling conflict. How many times have you heard terms such as "personality conflict" to describe a wide range of problematic situations in an organization? If nothing else, assessments like the MBTI allow managers to create an environment for employees that minimizes the unproductive wrangling over who's right and who's wrong. Our basic natures lead us to think that the way we are is normal and correct. Therefore, anyone not like us is wrong. That is, of course, not true, and employees need constant reminding of that, especially when in the throes of a personality conflict.

One of the most helpful statements we can make about conflict is that we do not want to eliminate it from the workplace. Conflict can be energizing, creative, and a real force for change and growth. It can also, of course, be destructive. The key for the effective manager is to be able to distinguish between the two.

Fighting over who is right and who is wrong is generally unproductive. Realizing that different perspectives exist and putting energy into combining ideas toward a creative solution is usually productive. Remind yourself and your staff: Different is not wrong; it is just different.

The Thinkers vs. the Doers: Part 2

In the example that began this chapter, Mike was worried about his staff meetings because accusations of hastiness and of foot-dragging were being exchanged on a regular basis. He was able to lessen the accusatory tone of the meetings by surfacing and devoting some time to what he had observed. Put in a nonjudgmental way, here is what he said:

"Greg and Karen seem comfortable acting on an amount of data that appears insufficient to George. George seems to prefer collecting more information before acting. From what I have seen, neither of these approaches is right; they are simply different. All three of you are very capable of making quality decisions."

He then stopped and asked his staff for feedback on what he had said so far. Once the members had agreed to this nonjudgmental view, he asked them to decide how they were going to resolve what amounted to a difference in the amount of information needed to make a decision comfortably. Mike facilitated some preliminary discussion and brought the issue up again at the beginning of the next few staff meetings so that staff members would realize that they were responsible for changing their behavior and that whatever way they chose was fine with Mike as long as meetings were productive and amicable.

Eventually, George took on the task of collecting data prior to meetings and presenting his findings in a concise way. Greg and Karen adjusted to his need to do this by giving him their agenda items ahead of time and not springing demands for decisions on him in a staff meeting and expecting an answer. All three parties became more comfortable with the team meetings and began slowly to appreciate the others' perspectives.

What Do You Need to Know About Personality?

Everyone has a personality, and no two are exactly alike. We have a tendency to think our personality is normal and that many other people's are a little bit tweaked. You (the manager) control some things in the organization (e.g., rewards and other consequences of people's behavior). Worry about those things. They will influence behavior (which is, of course, the very definition of management—getting things done through other people).

How do you influence attitudes or personality? You don't. You control only some of the consequences of people's behavior and can influence their behavior by using these consequences.

The overall message is that there are individual differences in people's personalities. As a manager, you can manage these differences; don't expect to change them. You can only influence and change behavior. We will talk more about this influence in Chapter 2.

Your concern as a manager is with people's behavior or performance, not with their personalities. Is personality related to job performance? That depends on the situation. Behavior is generally a function of the set of circumstances or the situation. Personality is a preferred style, a function of the traits a person possesses. While we can't predict someone's behavior from one specific situation to another, we can make general predictions over time.

An individual's personality definitely affects how much we like and trust the person. Be careful, however, not to confuse an employee's personality with her performance. As a manager, it is difficult for you to evaluate a person's performance in a vacuum. You will be influenced by personality, whether or not the personality influences the job performance.

Manager's Checklist

☐ Remember that you and the employees who work for you use defense mechanisms. They are unconscious and serve to reduce anxiety.

☐ People who feel good about themselves perform better. High self-esteem is a win-win for the company and for the employee.

☐ Personality, the situation, and the consequences of behavior interact constantly.

☐ Adaptability and flexibility—the ability to change with the situation—can be more important than any trait.

☐ Develop the ability to reflect honestly on your personality and behavior and their effect on those around you.

☐ Do everything you can to bolster your employees' confidence in themselves.

☐ Remind yourself and your staff: Different is not wrong; it is just different.

2

"Why Does He Keep Doing That?!" —*Learning and Behavior*

Although managers frequently talk about things like attitudes and personality conflicts, what they can most easily see, document, and manage is behavior. Behavior is defined as something specific and observable, thus moving managers away from unproductive conversations like:

"You're a slob."

"I am not."

and toward statements like:

"When you went home last night there were work papers, newspapers, and fast food wrappers all over the desk and floor in your cubicle."

Behavior that is rewarded increases in frequency. If there is a behavior occurring in your organization that you consider undesirable, find out how and why it is rewarding to people. Then you can either stop rewarding them for it or begin to reward an alternative behavior. This technique for modifying behavior assumes that all behaviors are learned, a concept that is the heart of this chapter. We will talk about learning theories and how learning leads to behavior.

The Contest: Part 1

Employees in a manufacturing firm were shipping unfinished or defect-ridden parts. Management responded by requiring supervisors to do more quality-control inspections. The problem continued, with employees becoming very innovative and creative at coming up with ways to ship defective parts.

Managers reacted to the situation in predictable ways. They talked about the decline of the work ethic, bemoaned the sabotage mentality of the employees, and began to develop ways to increase morale, starting with pizza parties at lunch and new team T-shirts.

Morale, however, was not the problem. (How often in organizations have we solved the wrong problem, only to see the situation continue or worsen!) The problem was a heavily promoted contest in which the team that shipped the most parts per month would be entered into a contest to win a cruise to the Bahamas. Far from having low morale, employees were excited about the cruise contest and made sure they qualified for the drawing by shipping more parts per month than any other team. This led, predictably and logically, to the shipping of defective parts.

This example presents a situation that is not unusual or even uncommon. Many actions that management undertakes have unintended effects, and the best-laid plans to reward performance backfire. Organizations will get what they ask for, so be careful what you ask for! Unfortunately, a reward system that takes all variables into account often becomes too complicated for employees to understand (and they have to understand it to find it motivating) or too complicated for the organization to administer.

In this chapter, we will talk about behavior; specifically, learned behavior, and how a general knowledge of behavioral principles can help managers avoid the unintended effects like those just described.

Classical Conditioning

You may have heard the story of Pavlov's dogs. Ivan Pavlov, a Russian physiologist, paired an attractive stimulus (food) with a neutral one (a bell ringing). The dogs were quickly conditioned to salivate at the sound of the bell, since they made the connection between the two. We humans, of course, have free will, and judgment, and conscience, and all of those fine things that keep us from salivating at the bell. Right? Wrong.

All behavior can be described as being caused by something. Even bizarre behavior can usually be explained. Think of the autistic character played by Dustin Hoffman in the movie *Rain Man*. His behavior was fairly bizarre by anyone's standards, yet when you understand autism, and what his behavior accomplished for him, it becomes understandable.

One of the most powerful conditioned stimuli in the workplace is the clock. Clock time is, of course, an invention. Numbers on a dial have nothing to do with our needs, wants, and desires. Yet at 10:00 A.M. on a workday, we want coffee. At noon, we go to lunch. Right at 3:00, the "need" for a candy bar or some chips kicks in. These are all conditioned responses, things that we learned to do over time as a result of some natural function being paired with an external stimulus.

Some workplace behaviors, of course, are not so harmless. There was a manager in an insurance firm who was having trouble with his assistant. She was an excellent employee, but occasionally she would leave her desk to chat with other employees and not be there to answer the phone. When the manager began to look at what might be causing the behavior, he first considered her personality (see Chapter 1). She was an extrovert who was extremely sociable and liked the company of others. The stimulus to the behavior of leaving her desk appeared to be the sight of groups of employees gathered around the water cooler, which was visible from her desk. She would hear a laugh or a few words of a conversation and be drawn to approach the group. The behavior (leaving her desk) was a response to a stimulus (the sight and sound of the small groups of people). The boss, wanting to save an otherwise good employee, simply moved her desk so that she could neither see nor hear what was going on in the hallway by the water cooler.

When you want to encourage or discourage a particular behavior in the workplace, look at the behavior in terms of its stimulus. It is particularly important to be able to identify the behaviors that contribute to the organization. People come to a job with a variety of skills and abilities. A graphic designer, for example, may have sketched for most of his life for the simple joy of drawing. At work, the organization pairs that skill (sketching) with a new stimulus (a paycheck), and the skill starts being performed for a new reason.

In the next section, we will consider the effects of another kind of conditioning, one that is useful when the employee does not already have the skills needed for the job.

Operant Conditioning

The well-known behavioral theorist B. F. Skinner rejected the notion that we could ever do anything more than speculate about what was going on in people's heads. Speculation, while perhaps enjoyable, is not very helpful in managing other people's behavior. Skinner suggested that people don't always just respond to stimuli, as Pavlov's dogs did, but that sometimes they actually emit behavior in the absence of a stimulus. These behaviors (called operants) are influenced by what happens afterward (the consequences).

In the previous section we looked at the idea that all behavior is caused by something. In this section we consider the consequences of behavior, the fact that all behavior has a purpose and that by managing the consequences we can influence the behavior.

Suppose you have an employee who failed to tell you about a critical customer problem. You discovered that the employee was hesitant to tell you about it because of your reputation for flying off the handle when faced with unpleasant news. Rather than risk such an unpleasant experience, the employee hid the problem from you. His behavior makes sense and can be explained by operant conditioning. A behavior (telling the boss about a problem) had an unpleasant consequence (being yelled at), so the employee learned to avoid the behavior. If you are being honest with yourself, who is to blame here? Even if you think you are just letting off steam and that the employee should understand that, try thanking him the next time he lets you know about a problem.

A similar, very common situation occurs when the boss delegates the responsibility for solving a problem to the person reporting it. Although this seems a great way to handle things, consider the fact that you may be conditioning your employees' behavior and keeping them from telling you about problems. In this case, the behavior (telling the boss about a problem) has a different negative consequence (being assigned extra work), but the result is still a decrease in the problem-reporting behavior.

I often tell students in my management classes that there are only four ways to influence behavior. They always look interested and begin to take careful notes, because students love it when you say anything like "Now, here are the four ways. . . ." There are, of course, very few simple explanations that really cover all the ground they claim to. But from a behaviorist's perspective, there really are only four ways to influence other people's behavior (and what is management but a constant attempt to influence other people's behavior?). There are two ways to increase a specific behavior (positive reinforcement and negative reinforcement) and two ways to decrease a specific behavior (punishment and extinction). Note that reinforcement, whether positive or negative, results in an increase in behavior; negative reinforcement is not the same as punishment. Let's consider each of the four techniques in turn.

Positive Reinforcement

If you have identified a specific behavior that you would like to have increase, a simple way to do that is to reward it. You have many options for positively reinforcing behavior on the job, including tangible things such as pay raises and plaques and intangibles such as praise.

There are two things to consider when offering positive reinforcement—the schedule of reinforcement and individual differences in what people find rewarding. Much of the research on schedules of reinforcement was performed on animals. Although animal studies may prove oversimplified when applied to humans, let's look first at the simple version; then we can complicate things with our second factor, individual differences.

Essentially, you can choose to reinforce behavior either continually or on some kind of schedule. If you reward a particular behavior each and every time it occurs, the behavior will increase very rapidly to a very high level. The problem with continual reinforcement in the workplace, of course, is that it is usually impossible! You cannot follow a single employee around all day and reinforce every instance of the desired behavior. Another drawback of continuous reinforcement is that as soon as you stop rewarding the behavior, the behavior quickly stops occurring as well.

If you decide to follow some kind of intermittent reinforcement, you will need to decide whether you will base reinforcement on elapsed time (an interval schedule) or on a certain number of instances of the behavior (a ratio schedule).

Fixed interval schedules involve rewarding the first behavior to take place after a set period of time elapses. Research shows that very little of the behavior will take place immediately after it is rewarded and that frequency will increase as the time approaches for another reward. Suppose you have an employee who is not following safety procedures and you want to positively reinforce his safe work practices. If you go down to the shop floor every day at 3:00 P.M. and reward the first instance you see of the employee following safety procedures, what do you think will happen to that employee's behavior each morning? The behavior decreases.

Variable interval schedules involve rewarding behavior at random time intervals. As you might expect, the behavior does not then show the drop-off that it does under fixed interval schedules. If you drop into the shop floor area at random times during the day, the employee's behavior will be much more uniform.

Fixed ratio schedules reward behaviors after the behavior has been performed a set number of times. If you were able to observe the shop employee over a period of time, for example, you could praise or thank him after each fifth episode of the specific "safe" behavior you were trying to influence. What generally tends to happen with fixed ratio schedules is that the rate of behavior drops off right after the reinforcement (because the employee knows he won't get another reward for a while), then picks up a burst of speed as the time for another reward approaches.

Variable ratio schedules reward behavior after a random number of occurrences. Variable ratio schedules provide the highest, most reliable rates of behavior of any of the schedules. Think about playing a slot machine at Las Vegas or Atlantic City. The payoff occurs after a random number of "plays." This variable ratio reward system results in a very high rate of behavior. In the shop employee example, varying both the time and the number of occurrences before you reinforce the behavior will produce the highest rate of behavior.

Negative Reinforcement

The term *negative reinforcement* is widely misunderstood. It is not the same thing as punishment, with which it is most frequently confused. It becomes easier if you think about what each of the two words means. *Negative* refers to the subtraction or removal of something from an equation. *Reinforcement* means that a behavior is rewarded in some way so that it continues.

Negative reinforcement, then, refers to the removal of an aversive stimulus so that the removal itself is rewarding. Suppose you wanted to teach a rat to press a bar located on one wall of its cage. You could give it a food pellet when it pressed that bar (positive reinforcement), or you could give it electric shocks unless it pressed the bar (negative reinforcement). In either case, the bar pressing behavior would continue or increase, which is why both tactics are called reinforcement.

Suppose that your employees really hate staff meetings. You have adopted a policy that says that if they meet their goals for the week, you will cancel that week's staff meeting. The behavior you are trying to influence (meeting goals) increases because an aversive stimulus (the staff meeting) has been removed. That is what negative reinforcement is all about.

Punishment

Punishment results in a decrease of the targeted behavior. It involves following an undesirable behavior with an aversive stimulus or with the removal of a pleasant stimulus. (Note that punishment, by this definition, can be either positive or negative, since those words are defined as giving something or taking something away.) There are a lot of issues, both ethical and practical, with using punishment in organizations. Let's explore a few of them.

Punishment does not make clear what the desired alternative behavior would be. Imagine that you are trying to housebreak your dog. When he urinates in the living room, you shout at him or swat him with a newspaper. The next time he feels the urge, he tries the dining room. Same response on your part. He now knows two places not to go but is no closer to the right answer than before. Taking him out to the yard at intervals, waiting for the behavior to occur naturally, and then praising and rewarding him will increase the desired behavior through positive reinforcement.

There are often undesirable side effects related to the use of punishment. Punishment may cause an employee to develop feelings of animosity toward you, the boss. Instead of connecting the punishment and the behavior, she may connect the punishment and you. In your absence, she may revert to the old behavior out of a desire to take revenge or even to sabotage your position in the company.

Punishment takes on authoritarian and parental overtones in organizations. It can be seen as dehumanizing and humiliating by employees, and it puts them in an unmistakably subordinate position. Think of the implications this would have should the employee be asked to join a discussion or a self-managed team or participate in the decision making for the department.

The fourth and final issue about punishment calls the first three into question, and that is that punishment works! It is an effective and fast-acting deterrent to undesirable behavior. Because of the drawbacks, however, it should be reserved for very serious infractions that need immediate correction.

As a manager, ask yourself if you have explored fully the reasons for the undesirable behavior. Ask yourself if you have, all unwittingly, been allowing the undesirable behavior to be rewarded (as in the organizational example that opened this chapter). Punishment is an option in cases where the behavior is so serious that it must be reacted to harshly. But realize that punishment is only one option of many available to you for influencing behavior, and that it carries the most undesirable side effects and should be seen as a tool of last resort.

Extinction

Extinction involves ceasing to reward behavior that was previously rewarded. The behavior then has a tendency to diminish, or become extinct. In animal research, if you teach a seal to jump through a hoop by giving it a fish each time it jumps and then quit giving it fish, it may jump through the hoop a few more times, but it will quickly learn that no fish are forthcoming and will stop jumping through the hoop. The behavior has become extinct. In organizations, of course, behavior is a little more complicated than that, in that most behavior is influenced by a variety of things. But you may be able to pick out one or two key rewards and stop them. If, for example, one of your employees tends to tell off-color jokes and you would like him to stop, quit rewarding the behavior by laughing. A hearty laugh, followed by a reminder that you want him to stop telling off-color jokes, is an ineffective way of stopping the behavior.

Individual Differences

Now we get to the place where we part company with the animal studies. A seal will jump through a hoop for a fish just as long as he is still somewhat hungry (which the trainer can control). An employee will not jump through hoops (literally or figuratively) if the "fish" is not something she desires. You have two choices here, depending on the number of people for whom you are responsible. If you have a relatively small staff, you can get to know something about each of them and what motivates them. For example, a request to work overtime can be seen as a reward (to the single parent struggling to make ends meet) or as a punishment (to the college student working for pocket money who has a "hot date"). If you have responsibility for a large group or for an entire company, you can go for the law of averages. Most people will find certain things rewarding. Offer a reward, and a certain percentage of the people working for you will respond. Offer a variety of rewards, and you increase your odds of hitting the majority of people.

The importance of understanding what motivates people cannot be overstated. We will go into this topic in more detail in Chapter 4.

Implications for Training in Organizations

When we manage learning, we are engaged in training. People in organizations are trained through their on-the-job experiences, as well as through formal training programs. To get the most out of your investment in training, the basic learning concepts need to be considered.

Does the employee already have the skills necessary for the job? If so, the organization simply needs to pair the desired behavior with a new stimulus (the paycheck). Does the employee need to learn a new skill? Training in organizations often involves learning new skills, and thus operant conditioning is a good model to use. When considering training, you might ask yourself just what it is you want your employees to learn. Do you simply need to communicate some kind of information to them? Is there a mental skill (e.g., problem solving) or a physical skill (e.g., operating a piece of equipment) to learn? Do you want them to learn an attitude, such as a commitment to customer service?

Communicating information to people is probably the easiest kind of training. It may simply require giving them a manual to read and then testing them on the concepts.

Physical skills are fairly easy to teach, as well. A common sequence of events is to demonstrate the action to the employee, have him do it, give him the opportunity to practice, and give him feedback on how he's doing or how to improve.

Mental skills are a little more difficult to teach, mostly because it is impossible to observe directly someone's cognitive processes. One way to observe a person as she applies a mental skill is to ask her to "think aloud" as she troubleshoots or solves a problem.

The most difficult kind of training attempts to change people's attitudes. Whether you are teaching line employees to care about the customer or teaching supervisors to care about the employees, you are working with deeply ingrained personalities and past behavior patterns. It is helpful to begin such training with some indication of why it is necessary for the organization and some evidence of what's in it for the employee. Simply teaching the "seven steps of effective interpersonal skills in supervision" without letting the supervisors know why they are important to the organization may be successful in a limited way (the supervisors can tell you what the seven steps are) but unsuccessful in the long run (the supervisors don't use the seven steps once they go back to work). A sequence of training that may be effective in teaching attitudes is to model the behavior for the trainees, allow them to practice the behavior, then provide for reinforcement once they perform the behavior on the job.

From what we have talked about so far in this chapter, it should be obvious that a traditional lecture-style classroom experience has some severe drawbacks when you are trying to change employees' behavior. Organizational training should, at the least, allow the learner to actively perform the new behavior, provide reinforcement for it, and offer follow-up to be sure that reinforcement is present on the job and gradually phased out (to prevent extinction). Now you see why trainers often insist on role playing during workshops! You may not have liked it and found it artificial and forced, but how else were you to learn the new behavior (whether it was a communication style, giving positive feedback, or giving a performance evaluation)? The biggest drawback to the transfer of training from the classroom to the job is the fact that the new behavior is not reinforced back on the job. Even if you are supported by a training department in your organization, you cannot simply send your employees to training and expect them to come back with new attitudes and behavior. You must provide an environment in which you model the desired behavior, allow them to practice it, and reinforce the behavior.

Think about the returns you want from your investment in training. For yourself, as well as for your staff, there are numerous costs involved in developing, delivering, and attending training in organizations. How often do we sit through a training class, think it all is just common sense, then promptly forget all about the "seven steps to effective interpersonal communication" the minute we get back to work?

Common sense or not, it is very difficult to change old patterns of behavior. It requires actually acting out the new behavior, first in practice sessions in the classroom, then back on the job. It also requires support back on the job. Don't throw your training budget away by thinking that a workshop on effective teamwork will somehow turn your staff into a high-performing team. Realistically, a workshop can only expose your staff to some principles of effective teamwork. It will not wave a magic wand over them and turn them into a high-performing team. You must be actively involved in requiring some new behaviors on the job and reinforcing them. Otherwise, your training dollars will be spent on a fun break from the daily routine or a boring obstacle to getting the job done, and no long-term behavior changes will be seen.

The Importance of Feedback

Feedback requires a few more words at this point. Feedback is essential to any type of new learning or behavior, because it provides an individual with direction (do I need to do this faster? slower? more to the right?). Giving your employees feedback requires that you be specific with both the positives and the negatives of what they are doing.

"Good job!" is not feedback. "This component was installed perfectly. You got just the right tension on the connectors and completed the job in ten minutes, which is just below the standard of eleven minutes" is feedback. For an employee to learn a behavior, he must be able to get direction from somewhere. Think about how your employees receive direction.

It is possible to get feedback internally. An equipment operator learns to tell by the feel of a lever if the right pressure is being applied. External feedback refers to anything coming from outside the individual, such as a supervisor's comments, a monthly sales report, or a setting on a gauge. Feedback can also be direct or indirect. In direct feedback, the employee observes or evaluates his own work (by way of the gauge, or the feel of the lever); indirect feedback is based on the observations of others (such as the comment from the supervisor). In general, the more feedback, the better. See how many ways you can help your employees receive feedback about how they are doing.

The Contest: Part 2

In the example that opened this chapter, we heard about the shipping clerks who shipped defective material because there were rewards in it for them. How can the principles of learning be applied to this situation?

The biggest learning here is that these people are not "bad," demoralized, or saboteurs. They are simply doing what the organization is rewarding them for doing. The reward system needs to be changed. Here are some options (if you need to, go back and review the case at the beginning of the chapter; then choose one of these alternatives):

1. Draft a policy stating that shipping any defective parts will disqualify that team from the contest.
2. Have a series of motivational meetings about the importance of quality to the organization's reputation.
3. Get feedback from customers on the number of defective parts shipped and subtract them from the team's totals.
4. Drop the contest.

Picked one? Let's look at them one by one.

The first option requires a lot of work on someone's part to check the quality of each shipment. Is it going to be worth all of the additional time and effort?

If you chose the second one, you haven't been listening! Remember, morale is not the issue. These employees are very motivated—to win the trip!

Would making the customer do more work benefit your organization and its reputation? The third option is not a good choice.

The fourth choice would be my advice. At the least, you need to change the rules of the contest so that number of parts shipped is not the only variable considered. You need to have systems in place that reward quality and quantity. Competition is generally not the way to go. Many factors may be influencing the behavior at this point, and dropping the contest may not be the only action you need to take, but it would be a good start.

What Do You Need to Know About Learning?

How do you combine classical and operant conditioning theories of learning to help you be a better manager? If you think about them as two sides to the same coin, it is simple. It all has to do with how behavior is learned.

Look at a behavior that you would like to change in the workplace. Let's use the example we talked about earlier, the one in which one of your employees habitually tells off-color stories and jokes in the lunchroom. You would like him to stop before another employee takes offense. You can look at the behavior first from the Pavlovian or stimulus-response theory and ask, "What is causing this behavior?" If you can identify and remove the stimulus, the behavior should extinguish itself. Maybe the off-color jokes occur only when a particular person is in the room who waits expectantly for the story.

You can also look at the behavior from the Skinnerian or operant conditioning approach. Instead of looking at what happens before the behavior (the stimulus), you can look at what happens immediately after the behavior (the consequence). If you have told the person to stop and he continues doing the undesirable, you can assume that there is some other consequence to the behavior that he finds rewarding. Perhaps everyone laughs, and he loves the attention. Let's look at the four ways of influencing behavior that we talked about earlier:

1. *Extinction.* If you can identify the rewarding consequence, you can remove it. In this example, you need the cooperation of the others in the group. You also need to watch any conflicting messages you yourself are sending—do you laugh when the jokes are told (maybe a little uncomfortably)?
2. *Punishment.* You can also substitute an unrewarding consequence. Perhaps you decide that every time you hear the off-color stories, you will reprimand or otherwise punish the wrong-doer.
3. *Positive reinforcement.* When the desired behavior occurs (perhaps a coffee break has gone by and the person has not told off-color jokes), reward that alternative behavior by any means that are available to you. Praise the person, thank him,

give him the rest of the day off, or otherwise signal to him that this is the behavior that you want and expect.

4. *Negative reinforcement.* Remember, reinforcement causes behavior to increase. The behavior you want increased here is the coffee break or lunch period that goes by with no off-color jokes. Negative (meaning you take something away) reinforcement means that something the person doesn't like (e.g., being yelled at, written up) doesn't happen!

Manager's Checklist

☐ Behavior is caused by something (a stimulus).

☐ Behavior has consequences, and later behavior is a function of these consequence.

☐ You can influence behavior by managing consequences.
  • Reward the behavior.
    —Give a reward (positive reinforcement).
    —Take away something the person dislikes (negative reinforcement).
  • Ignore the behavior (extinction).
  • Follow the behavior with something the person dislikes (punishment).

☐ Define what it is you want your employees to learn.
  • Information
  • Mental skill
  • Physical
  • Attitude

☐ Define the appropriate training.
  • Manuals
  • Classroom training
  • Demonstrations
  • Practice
  • Feedback
  • Reinforcement

3

"I Know What I Saw" —*Perception*

There is a great deal of research on the physiology of perception—the visual system, the brain, the auditory mechanisms. In this section, we are not as concerned with how information is transmitted to the brain (sensation) as we are with our attempts to understand and make sense of the information (perception).

Perception has a huge influence on behavior. What makes perception so fascinating is that there is no such thing as "reality." As you will see, so many things influence perception that there are seldom two people who will look at the same situation and agree on what it means. What are the implications for managing people in organizations? As we attempt to understand and influence behavior at work, we need to consider the role of all of the factors that influence perception.

The Boss's Bad Mood: Part 1

Imagine that you are having one of those mornings. Your day-care provider was ill, and you had to make several calls to neighbors and friends in order to make other arrangements for the care of your three-year-old. The dog threw up on your shoes as you grabbed a quick cup of coffee in the kitchen. The commute was more nerve-wracking than usual, including a close call with a teen-aged driver who cut into your lane without looking.

None of your staff is aware of these events. Here is what they see: The boss comes in scowling, goes straight into his office without the usual morning greetings, and shuts the door behind him.

By 10:00, there have been numerous conversations about the meaning of this behavior. One of the staff read an article in yesterday's newspaper about a local investor who is looking to buy companies. In the speculation about "what's wrong," this particular piece of information takes on a life of its own. By noon, it is being circulated on the grapevine as a fact: The company has been sold, the boss is losing his job, and countless others will follow him to the unemployment line in the months to come.

Perception in the Workplace

Communication takes place in organizations in a variety of ways. In fact, just about everything about an organization communicates something. This includes verbal and nonverbal messages, the layout of the office space, the color the building is painted, what hangs on the walls, who goes on coffee break with whom . . . you get the idea. The organizational climate is made up of a whole series of perceptions, perceptions that may or may not have anything to do with what the organization intended to communicate. Perceptions lead each of us to make inferences and assumptions, which become our reality. We will discuss communication at length in Chapter 9, but an understanding of perception must come first.

Perception is influenced by day-to-day events, as in the example just given. It is also influenced by past experience, expectations, interests, emotional state, motives, and personality. In this chapter we will discuss some of the ways perception can be better understood and how that understanding can help us manage other people in the workplace. A brief discussion of each of these general concepts of perception follows:

- Attention
- Adaptation
- Motives
- Expectations
- Pattern perception
- Cognitive styles
- Perceptual hypotheses
- Signal detection
- Human factors
- Selective perception

Attention

We do not and cannot pay attention to everything. Attention refers to the fact that we simply filter out a great deal of what goes on around us although it is readily available for us to perceive.

What gets filtered out, and what gets our attention? At the most basic levels (leaving out, for a moment, selective perception), things that stand out from the background noise attract our attention. Stimuli that are louder, brighter, or larger get our attention. In addition, we pay more attention to unexpected stimuli.

You may have seen, or used, many desperate attempts to get attention in written memos. In organizations where information comes in deluges and in-boxes are jammed, there are some common ways of attempting to get a memo to stand out. Have you ever skipped the white memo paper and used colored paper, or even some of the newer neon shades? When people don't read their mail, bolding, underlining, and using larger fonts are all used in efforts to get people to pay attention and to tell them "This memo needs your attention!" You may have borrowed some power from above and asked your boss to send the message under her signature.

The unexpected also gets our attention. If you have been listening to your voice mail with half an ear, only to snap awake at the sound of the CEO's voice, you are familiar with this phenomenon.

We can pay attention to more than one thing at a time (thank goodness!). Most workplaces require that we pay a great deal of attention to many different stimuli. When trying to get people's attention, keep in mind the atmosphere within which they work. If the office is a quiet place and most of the stimuli are written (paper memos and E-mail), an auditory signal will be easier to combine with all the written stimuli. Most of us can drive and listen to the car radio at the same time, because the signals coming in require different types and levels of attention.

Keep the attention factor in mind in your own communications in the office. Most of us are bombarded with information. You will need some true attention-getting tactics to cause your message to stand out from the noise. Once you have gotten people to attend to you, the other variables discussed in this chapter will begin to influence what happens to the message.

Adaptation

The concept of adaptation tells us that continued exposure to a particular stimulus leads to a lessened sensitivity to that stimulus. In other words, while the first bite of your meal tastes delicious, your response to it lessens as you continue eating, and not just because you begin to get full. When you walk into a room and smell a foul odor, within a very few minutes you adjust. We evolved this way because changing stimuli were more important to pay attention to than continuing stimuli, for our protection and survival. As we said in the previous section, we simply cannot pay attention to everything.

What is the importance of the adaptation principle to the workplace? When you really want to get someone's attention, change the stimulus! If your usual style is a fairly loud and blustery tone, the people who work for you have adapted to it. You may get more attention by speaking softly. If you usually communicate by E-mail, send a written memo. A new stimulus, whatever that is in your organization, will get attention. Partly because of this principle, an important strategic planning meeting may be scheduled "off-site" in an effort to get away from all the usual stimuli and get people to pay attention.

The bottom line is that when you have a serious message to communicate, change your usual style, whatever that happens to be. That way, the message will receive more attention.

Motives

Our current state of motivation, our needs and desires, distorts our perceptions. If the need is strong enough, it can even determine our perception. If you have skipped lunch, for example, you notice the fast-food restaurants on your drive home; if your gas gauge is on Empty, you pay more attention to the gas stations on your route.

We will devote an entire chapter to motivation (see Chapter 4), but suffice it to say that taking the motivational levels of people into account when you want to influence them is critical. If you offer inducements that people neither want nor need, they will be ineffective. If you threaten people with termination in a company with a long history of never firing anyone, you will not get their attention.

If you have been in a fairly unproductive staff meeting all morning, and it is a quarter to twelve, announcing that you will not break for lunch unless the agenda is finished may spur some very productive work. Making the same announcement at 8:00 A.M. will not have nearly as powerful an effect.

Do not underestimate the power of this kind of distortion. As with all of the psychological principles we are talking about, the biggest lesson is that it applies to you as well! If you need a report to get to your boss by 4:00 P.M. and one of your employees hands it to you at 3:50, your need to get it turned in will distort your ability to judge the acceptability of the product. You will literally look at it differently than you would if the employee had handed it to you at 9:00 A.M.

As we will see in Chapter 4, some motives are transitory (like hunger), and some are fairly fixed (like the need for power). Your internal, fixed needs, such as your needs for power and achievement, will influence your perception of things like job offers, project opportunities, and annual evaluations. If you have a high need for power, you may accept a promotion into a managerial role even though you really like the technical work you do. You may miss the "hands-on" work, but you will justify your decision in your mind by perceiving the promotion as more desirable than the objective observer might.

When you attempt to influence the behavior of your employees, keep in mind that they are a constantly shifting mass of needs and motives, some transitory and some fixed, all of which will affect your ability to influence them. No wonder management can be difficult!

Expectations

Our expectations also influence our perception and help determine where we give our attention. There are two major learnings here: We perceive what we expect to perceive, and the unexpected gets our attention far more quickly than the expected.

You expect to see an elephant in a zoo and will pay the requisite amount of attention to it. You do not expect to see an elephant in your backyard and will pay a much greater amount of attention to it there. To save ourselves from having to pay attention to everything (which we have already established is impossible), we generalize our perceptions into that which is familiar to us. What does that mean?

It may sound simplistic to say that we perceive what we expect to perceive, but in fact expectations are a powerful influence on our perception and thus our behavior. One day I encountered my sister at a neighborhood store. She was accompanied by a small girl whom I expected to be my niece, and thus I perceived her as such. It was not until the end of the conversation, when I said my good-byes and added, "Good-bye, Dayna" that they looked at me oddly. My sister said, "This isn't Dayna." It was, in fact, a neighbor's child. I perceived what I expected to perceive and, until that moment, would have sworn in a court of law that I had seen Dayna that day. Makes you wonder about eyewitness testimony, doesn't it?

Of far more interest to organizations is the effect expectations have on productive work on the job. Our expectations, and those of the people around us, have a far-reaching effect on our actions and interactions. Suppose you have had a few annoying conversations with a new employee. You have come to expect (very quickly) that this employee will be long-winded and irrelevant when he contributes to a conversation. Guess what? You perceive what you expect, and every time this employee opens his mouth, you act as if what he says is of no value. You can imagine the effect this has on his career. This concept is similar to that of the self-fulfilling prophecy.

The idea behind the self-fulfilling prophecy is that if we believe something about ourselves or someone else, we tend to behave in ways that bear out our belief. If we believe that we are going to fail, why should we try very hard? Then, of course, because we didn't try, we fail. In the case of an employee, someone you want and need to influence, you have an impact on the perceptions of that employee. Consider the value of having employees who perceive that they are winners and hard workers. These perceptions cause them to act like winners and hard workers. If you believe and act as if your employees are lazy, untrustworthy, and not too bright, these beliefs will also tend to be reflected in the employees' performance. There is a great deal of research that shows the incredible power of the self-fulfilling prophecy. In one study, when teachers were told that a particular group of children (actually randomly chosen) were bright, these children actually showed an improvement in IQ over the course of the school year. In another study, supervisors were told that several new employees (also randomly chosen) were quick learners; these employees in fact excelled at the new-hire training. Your perceptions about people affect their performance, and their perceptions about themselves also affect their performance.

So if you want superior performance from your employees, you have a few choices. The direct approach (exhorting people to work hard, arranging for rewards and punishments) is time-consuming and doesn't always work. The internal approach (creating an environment where employees perceive themselves as hard workers) is cheaper, as well as more effective. As we will see in Chapter 4, external motivators are not nearly as effective as internal or intrinsic motivators.

Pattern Perception

As we begin learning to make sense of the bombardment of sensation that surrounds us, one of the tools we use is called pattern perception. We begin to be able to perceive basic elements of a stimulus (it has four legs, is hairy, and barks) and are then able to perceive it as a complete object (a dog). Perceiving the object requires that we match it to objects in our memory; if it is not a perfect match, we categorize it by matching it to something that comes close. (Thus, we recognize a nonbarking dog as a dog, nonetheless.)

The most fascinating observations of pattern perception come from watching small children trying to make sense of the world around them. If a child is familiar with dogs, she may refer to cats as dogs the first time she sees a cat. I recently heard a small child tell her mother, "Look! An ant!" when she spotted a fly on the window. Her pattern perception of insects had not yet broadened much beyond the ants she saw in the yard every day. "That's a fly, honey," said the mother. "And will it sting me?" asked the child, since she had some knowledge of bees and was still trying to find a category for the fly.

In the workplace, we all develop pattern perceptions that are in many cases a result of the career specialty we have chosen. When a new project is announced, an accountant may want to add up the numbers, a human resources manager may want to know the effect on people, and a marketing analyst will want data on possible customer bases. These pattern perceptions are extremely helpful in combination and help a team see the big picture. The trick for a manager is to make sure that each person is not so deeply embedded in her perception that she fails to recognize or appreciate the richness brought to the project by taking everyone's perception into account. Recognize your own patterns of perception, recognize that your own view is only one piece of the pattern, and cultivate teamwork that can take alternate views of reality into account.

Cognitive Styles

We have all developed our own particular styles of viewing the world. We have our own distinctive methods for dealing with the world and its input and for categorizing and making sense of the input.

There are people, for example, who see things as mostly similar. They perceive the similarities among categories of things (e.g., "animals," "coworkers"). There are others who see things in much more detail and tend to think in categories (e.g., "dogs and cats," "men and women").

There are people who think in terms of the big picture and people who think in terms of the details. (One group sees the forest, one the trees.) There are people who put a lot of weight on logic and "the facts," and other people who prefer to rely on feelings and emotions to guide their behavior.

For the manager, the implication here is that you probably need all different types of cognitive styles to work effectively in organizations. The fit between the person and the job would be affected if, for example, a very global thinker was assigned to a very detail-oriented task. Instead of trying to fit a square peg into a round hole, let people gravitate toward jobs they are good at, and, when putting together a team, make sure that different styles are represented. This is more difficult than it sounds, a point we address in various other chapters when group behavior is discussed. Different cognitive styles find each other irritating. They may have to be taught to appreciate the different perspectives that others bring.

Perceptual Hypotheses

Many of the perceptual mechanisms that we have discussed to this point work together to create perceptual hypotheses, the inferences and assumptions without which we could not function in the world. We almost always must make do with less than complete information, so we take the information we do have and form hypotheses about the world around us. We have this ability because we can't wait until all information is in before we make a decision. It is a very helpful ability, as long as we don't confuse our hypotheses with reality. Unfortunately, we often do.

Our perceptual hypotheses are often quite accurate. They are also sometimes wrong. Many popular optical illusions are the result of incorrect perceptual hypotheses. In the workplace, of course, the implications are more serious. Our hypotheses are real to us, so we act as if they are, creating the potential for conflict. There are also consequences for agreement, consensus, and smooth teamwork in organizations.

As we have seen, our wishes, needs, and biases all influence what we perceive. And, as we saw in Chapter 1, we are unaware of our own biased views of reality because our defenses keep many of our biases unconscious. Life experiences, such as growing up in different cultures, also affect our perceptions.

Suppose that your staff is asked to make a decision on the basis of sketchy details. You don't have time to collect more data; the situation requires action. Each individual on your staff, depending upon his background, his mood, and his cognitive style, will put the information together a little differently and will come to his own individual conclusion about the correct course of action. You can choose to engage in a long and fruitless discussion about who is right and who is wrong, or you can creatively put all of the pieces together to take advantage of all the different viewpoints.

Signal Detection

We detect stimuli from our environment in a variety of ways. We also filter out many stimuli. How do we decide what to pay attention to?

What we focus our attention on has been called the *figure,* with all else going on around us known as the *ground.* We can fairly easily switch our attention from figure to ground, as shown by the common experience of having a conversation in a crowded room or at a party. We are usually able to concentrate fairly well on the person we are talking to, but if someone mentions our name in a nearby conversation, all of a sudden our attention is diverted.

How well do we detect the signals around us? One variable is the importance of the stimulus. If you are waiting for a call from the hospital telling you how the surgery on your child went, you will be hypersensitive to the phone ring.

What kinds of implications are there in signal detection errors? You might mistakenly believe that a signal is present (thinking you hear the phone ring while you are watching television and answering it, to hear only a dial tone) or not hear a signal that is present (the phone is ringing, but you don't hear it because you are engrossed in your TV program). In the workplace, a great deal of attention may be given to preventing either of these kinds of errors, depending on the magnitude of the consequences. A worker in a nuclear power plant cannot afford to miss a signal that something is going wrong. In such cases, a gauge may be combined with an auditory signal (a siren), as well as with a visual signal (flashing lights).

Overload is an important consideration in designing a workplace that is sensitive to signal detection errors. During the first few minutes of the malfunction at the Three Mile Island nuclear plant in 1979, more than one hundred alarms went off. There was no way to pick out the important signals and get an immediate grasp of the situation. The necessary information was not presented in a way that made it clear to the employees what actions needed to be taken.

Human Factors

There is an entire body of knowledge that goes into what is known as human factor engineering. Workers in nuclear power plants are probably surrounded by equipment that was designed with many of the perceptual principles in mind. Human factors are taken into account in the design of assembly lines, cockpits, and dashboards. Although "ergonomics" has come to refer to the design of products with worker safety and comfort in mind (e.g., ergonomic chairs, computer keyboards, wrist supports), it behooves the designers to know about things like the threshold levels for attention getting and other perceptual concept.

Human factors come into play during three different phases of employee information interaction: the point at which the employee receives the information, the processing of the information, and the action that the employee takes on the basis of the information.

In the workplace, we devise many types of ways in which to display information to employees. Written materials, various types of signals, clocks, and other displays all serve to provide information. When you want to send an employee a signal to do something, you have many choices as to how to present the signal. Your decision ought to rest on what you know about the demands that are already made on the employees' senses and the advantages of one type of signal over another.

In a loud workplace (a manufacturing plant), for example, a great amount of demand is already put on employees' auditory (hearing) capability. You may choose to install a signal that is visual, such as a flashing light. When you consider the advantages of one type of signal over another, it is also important to keep the work environment in mind. A visual signal (e.g., a flashing light) requires that the employee look at it for it to be perceived and thus may be inferior to an auditory signal (e.g., a siren) unless the employee habitually directs her attention to the location of the visual signal.

The second phase to be considered in human factors is the internal process that the employee goes through once she has received the information. In a split second, she will evaluate the information, compare it to past experience, and make a judgment as to what to do next. As a manager, you need to be clear on what you are asking employees to do with this information. Are you asking her to react to the signal and take some specific, predetermined action? Or are you asking her to evaluate the signal and make a decision as to the correct course of action? Either choice requires training and clear communication of expectations. If time is critical—if, for example, a siren indicates that she has ten seconds to fix a potential problem or a disaster will result—there will probably need to be predetermined courses of action and training in advance. If accuracy of response is of major concern, time is of less concern, and there are many possible courses of action, you may be asking the employee to make a decision and thus require her to know a great deal about possible courses of action and their ramifications.

Third, after the employee has received a signal and processed it, she must take action on the basis of her decision or reaction. The action may entail making a physical change (flipping a switch, adjusting a dial) or taking action to communicate with someone else (calling 911, evacuating the building, making an entry in a log book).

When designing various types of signaling devices in your workplace, remember that the unexpected signal that is perceived as important and that has not been adapted to is the one most likely to get an employee's attention.

Selective Perception

The perceptual concept that has the biggest influence on the workplace is selective perception. All of us are highly selective in what we choose to pay attention to. We are bombarded with information, so we filter much of it out. The categorization processes we engage in allow us to simplify and make sense of this bombardment. The downside of this is that we screen out information that is incompatible with our beliefs, expectations, and desires.

Selective perception happens to everyone, and it happens all the time. You will not get rid of it in your work group, nor will you convince people that they are wrong. Instead of spending frustrating amounts of time trying to get people to see things differently, accept the fact that you cannot be completely objective about any situation, but you can be aware of the selective perception that is pervasive in your work group (and every other work group). Part of understanding other people is understanding that there is really no such thing as a right or wrong viewpoint. A perception is simply an individual's view of a situation, based on that individual's personality, upbringing, and previous experiences.

The Boss's Bad Mood: Part 2

In the organizational example that opened this chapter, you saw that other people's perception of your actions has a far greater impact on what is communicated than your intentions do. We talked about your reaction to a series of crises unrelated to the business day. You will undoubtedly have days like this (not often, you hope), and you cannot remain unaffected by these events. You can, however, become aware that your behavior will be perceived by people and interpreted by them. Their interpretation of events is what is going to drive their behavior, not your intentions.

It is also critical to keep in mind that you, too, engage in selective perception. Your understanding of psychological concepts is incomplete if it does not include the realization that they apply to you, as well as to the people around you. An academic understanding of concepts like selective perception is one thing; a true appreciation of how it applies to you is the real value.

What Do You Need to Know About Perception?

There are limits to the amount of information we can take in. Every person has developed ways of dealing with this limitation by filtering the sensations received into a perceptual pattern. You can begin to see why discussions about the reality of a situation can be unproductive, frustrating, and in fact often useless. Instead of trying to convince someone of the rightness of your view, agreeing to disagree and moving on can be quite productive.

Manager's Checklist

- ☐ *Attention.* Things that stand out from the background noise attract our attention. Stimuli that are louder, brighter, larger, or unexpected will be noticed more.

- ☐ *Adaptation.* Continued exposure to a stimulus (like the boss shouting at you) results in adaptation, or paying less attention to that stimulus. To get attention, change your usual ways of communicating.

- ☐ *Motives.* Needs and desires distort people's perceptions. Expect it, and work with it. Use the detailed information in Chapter 4 to help.

- ☐ *Expectations.* We perceive what we expect to perceive. Obviously, this can be either positive or negative. Be aware of your own expectations about your employees, and work to create an atmosphere within which their expectations are positive.

- ☐ *Pattern perception.* We perceive basic elements of stimuli and are then able to perceive them as complete objects. Every person may arrive at a somewhat different conclusion. Don't worry so much about right and wrong; cultivate teamwork that can take alternative views of reality into account.

- ☐ *Cognitive styles.* We have all developed a particular style of viewing the world. As was the case with pattern perception, the effective manager uses the different styles to create synergy, rather than allow the different styles to lead to unproductive conflict.

- ☐ *Perceptual hypotheses.* Much of what we perceive, and base our actions on, are inferences and assumptions.

Sometimes our assumptions are accurate, and sometimes they are not. The biggest lesson for a manager is to realize that this is true about himself and that he must therefore be open to alternative explanations of events or decisions.

☐ *Signal detection theory.* When designing the workplace, keep in mind the implications of missing a signal or mistakenly believing that a signal is present when it is not.

☐ *Human factors.* When analyzing your workplace from a perception point of view, human factors would encourage you to look at three places: the point at which the employee receives information, the process of the information, and the action that the employee takes based on the information.

☐ *Selective perception.* Be aware of the selective perception in your work group. These perceptions are based on each individual's personality, upbringing, and previous experience and will not change even if you present a brilliantly logical argument as to why your perception is correct and the employee's is not.

4

"How Can I Get People to Do What I Want Them to Do?" —*Motivation*

Few "people management" issues are of greater interest to managers than motivation. We talk loosely about employees being "unmotivated" but rarely take a close look at what we can do to change the motivational environment.

Remember what we said about behavior in Chapter 2—that it is caused, that it has a purpose, and that it is not a mystery. The heart of all behavior is motivation, and in this chapter we will wrestle with questions that are dear to managers' hearts: Why do people do what they do? Why don't they do what you want them to do? And how can you more effectively influence what they do?

The Process Improvement Team: Part 1

Imagine an organization that has always prided itself on being a great place to work. It sponsored picnics for employees' families every summer and frequent holiday parties. Various departments were always buying team T-shirts, pizza, raffle prizes, or other morale-boosting items. Yet morale at this company was not high. Employee surveys showed that, while most employees were not actively unhappy, they were not really thrilled about their jobs or the company.

When the organization implemented Total Quality Management, a series of classes was offered, including one about process improvement teams. For the purposes of the class, teams were put together and given a "real-life" process to improve. The teams were cross-level and cross-functional, so they included a broad cross-section of employees from all levels of the organization.

The work done by the teams was done in addition to all of their normal duties. In the four weeks they were given to complete their projects, the teams met, worked, fought, cried, and came up with astonishing results. Long-term employees who had not liked their jobs for years were doing work at home on the weekends for their teams. Clerical employees who could point to little in the way of accomplishments collared people continually to tell them about "my team."

The Needs That Motivate Behavior

There is an interesting group of drives in every human being that determines how we interact with the world around us. The basic survival drives, like the need for food and water, are not as evident in the workplace as some of our other instincts—our need for activity, curiosity, and manipulation.

People need to be active. The level of activity we seek differs tremendously, but, generally, people dislike being confined in a small space with nothing to do. People also have a drive to explore new and unknown places and stimuli. We have a preference for complexity over simplicity, because complexity is more interesting. We also have a tendency to enjoy manipulation; we want to touch, play with, and handle specific objects. These very basic needs have far-reaching implications for the design of jobs and of workplaces. No wonder boring, repetitive, or "make-work" jobs, even if they are easy, lead to burnout, frustration, and even sabotage (just to "liven things up"!).

The best-known name in the motivation field is Abraham Maslow. Academic courses and management training seminars alike tout Maslow's hierarchy of needs as the answer to motivating people in organizations. ("You've heard of Maslow?" I asked one management training group. "Oh yeah, the triangle guy!" said one participant.)

Theories, Maslow's and others, are helpful only if they help managers predict behavior and give them some tools to influence behavior. In this section, theories about the needs that motivate behavior will be explored with an eye to answering the question "How does this help me manage people?"

Maslow's theory states that unmet needs motivate behavior. Our needs are arranged in a hierarchy; the more basic needs must be satisfied before the higher-order needs will kick in and begin motivating our behavior. The five levels of needs, from the bottom up, are physiological or survival needs (food, water), safety needs (shelter), social needs (belongingness, love, acceptance), esteem needs (self-esteem and the esteem of other people), and self-actualization (self-development and the realization of potential).

Of what value is the hierarchy of needs in motivating people at work? One of the basic lessons of the theory is that appealing to a need that is already met or to a need that is at a level higher than that of an existing unmet need does not motivate behavior. Suppose you approached a homeless person with the following proposition: "I've got a job for you! It doesn't pay much; in fact, it's volunteer work. But you are going to be able to help other people and really make a contribution to society." Most likely, your pitch will fall on deaf ears. The homeless person will be far more likely to respond to an offer of manual labor that will result in enough money to allow him to eat that day. You are appealing to a need that is higher than an unmet need. For an example of an appeal to needs that are already met, suppose you approached an independently wealthy person and said, "I've got a job for you! It's somewhat of a drudgery, but it does pay a decent wage, enough to keep a roof over your head." In this case, too, your offer is unlikely to be accepted. In both examples, your motivating efforts will fail because you are appealing to needs that are on different levels from the individual's unmet needs.

Think about the people who make up the workforce of the average organization. Most of them are not starving or homeless. Most of them have at least some semblance of safety and security. And what do we offer them as motivators? Pay. Benefits. Retirement plans. These things get them in the door but do not continue to get them out of bed in the morning and into work with a commitment that benefits the organization. What kinds of things do foster commitment? The hierarchy tells us that most people have at least some of their social needs met. We have families, friends, neighbors, church groups. Some people have social needs that are met through work, however. We spend a lot of time at work, and sometimes our social circle is drawn from our co-workers. So the coffee breaks, water cooler chitchat, and social conventions that go on in organizations do have their place, no-nonsense managers to the contrary.

At the next level, esteem needs, we know that for

most of us, at least some of these needs are unmet. (Maslow said that no one reaches the self-actualizing level and stays there; at best, we can hope to reach that point a few times in our lives, only to drop back.) So the need for self-esteem and the esteem of others is a significant motivating factor in most people's lives. This single fact is the most valuable lesson that managers can draw from Maslow's theory.

People have a need to feel good about themselves and the work they do. People also have a need to feel recognized by others for the work they do. This is not "warm-fuzzy, feel-good" advice that managers can dismiss. This is a fact that should encourage managers to create an environment that allows for the release of motivation in a way that leads to a committed workforce composed of people whose hearts and minds, not just their hands, are applied to the job.

For some reason, this fairly simple fact is difficult to get across to some managers. An old-style, autocratic, "I am the boss" attitude, an attitude of "They get paid; what more do they want?," is more prevalent than we would like to think. This attitude works, insofar as it gets compliance from people. Think of the organizational implications of getting more than compliance, however, for getting true commitment. This is what Maslow's theory has to offer managers. Recognizing effort and making it possible for employees to maintain and enhance their self-esteem have such profound impacts and are so easy and inexpensive that it is puzzling that they are not more widely used.

There were a few other motivational theorists who attempted to outline the needs that motivate behavior. Most of their concepts are variations on Maslow's theory, with the added opinion that the strict hierarchy is not necessary. Clayton Alderfer, for example, suggested that there were really only three levels of need: existence, relatedness, and growth. David McClelland used other names for the needs, calling them power, achievement, and affiliation. But the researcher who was the most influential in designing organizations and jobs to be more motivating was Frederick Herzberg.

Herzberg found that there were two factors involved in the motivation to work. He called one factor, roughly analogous to Maslow's first two levels, the "hygiene factors." These factors involve the *context* in which the work is performed and include things like salary, working conditions, and job security. The second set of factors is the motivators; these involve the *content* of the job, or the work itself. Motivators are things like achievement, recognition, and responsibility.

Herzberg is famous for saying, "If you want someone to do a good job, give them a good job to do." In other words, before you spend a lot of time worrying about how to motivate people, examine the job you are asking them to do and see if you can make it more worth doing. If you ask someone to do a boring and pointless job, he will be bored and feel pointless. What does this tell us about the way we design jobs in the first place?

Using Herzberg's findings, it becomes obvious that the more autonomy you can build in to a job, the more an employee will feel some sense of responsibility. An employee also needs to feel that her task has some significance; a manager can present the "big picture" to her staff members and show them the significance of their tasks in the larger scheme of things. To feel a sense of achievement, employees also need feedback so that it is clear to them how well they are doing or, if they are not doing so well, how they can make corrections.

The lessons Herzberg has to offer managers involve what is known as job enrichment: Make the job as interesting as possible, and build in some variety, some autonomy, plenty of feedback, and a sense of the significance of the task. That may mean giving up a little of the managerial control that many of us are so fond of. But the payback in committed employees who enjoy their work will far exceed the investment in redesigning the job.

How Is Behavior Energized?

In addition to the theories that tell us what needs motivate behavior, there is another group of theories that explore how behavior is energized. Once a need motivates a certain behavior, what direction will the behavior take? What choice will the employee make in meeting the need? Once again, the basic question to be considered is: What in these theories is of value to the practicing manager? In this section, we will explore expectancy theory, equity theory, and goal setting.

One way to explain motivated behavior is through *expectancy theory*. Expectancy theory states that we are thoughtful decision makers who decide among alternative courses of action by picking the one action that seems most to our advantage. Consider a sales manager who tries to motivate behavior by telling the salespeople on his staff that if they sell one hundred widgets this month they will get a trip to the Bahamas. The salespeople will then decide how hard they are going to work by weighing three factors: how much they value the outcome (the trip), whether the outcome is associated with performance on the job ("If I work really hard, will I get the trip, or will they figure out a way to rig the contest so the boss's pet wins, as usual?"), and whether it is possible to reach the goal ("If I really work hard, is it even possible to sell one hundred?").

When trying to motivate behavior, a manager needs to ask: Do employees value the reward I'm giving?

Would they prefer something else? A woman confided in me once that she was embarrassed about winning a trip to the Bahamas. Although the airfare and hotel were paid for, food and other expenses for the week were not. She and her husband took the trip and were put in a financial bind by the additional expenses, but she felt she would appear ungrateful if she either turned down the trip or explained to her boss why she didn't want to go.

The second question is: Are the rewards I'm offering associated with good performance, and do employees see the connection? Many bonus plans fail to pass this test. Many employees have said, about their quarterly or annual bonuses, that they have no idea how much they're getting or why. They simply receive or don't receive a check in varying amounts. If the bonus system is too convoluted, it does not motivate behavior because employees do not perceive the connection.

The third question is: Are employees capable of and trained to do the jobs they are assigned? If employees cannot do what you ask of them, motivational efforts will fall flat. Only if all three of these factors are in place—an outcome employees value, a perceived connection between performance and rewards, and a perception among employees that they can do the job—will the motivational effort succeed as planned.

Equity theory is a little simpler than expectancy theory. According to equity theory, if employees see a discrepancy between their efforts and their rewards, they will try to reduce the discrepancy. There are essentially two ways to reduce the discrepancy: changing the effort or changing the reward. Most employees have more control over their efforts than over the level of rewards, so will seek to strike a balance by making more or less of an effort on the job. Since equity theory involves comparing oneself to someone else, it has a greater effect on the amount of cooperation among workers. This will be discussed in greater detail in Chapter 7.

There is one more school of thought about the choices that energize our behavior, and that is *goal-setting theory*. According to goal-setting theory, the rewards we offer people and the incentive plans we develop are useful in motivating people only if they lead to goal setting.

Goals provide an end point toward which to direct behavior. To reach a goal, an individual must receive feedback on how well he is progressing toward the goal. A manager's job consists largely of giving people enough information so that they can work harder, work at different things, relax, or renegotiate the goals. The implication for a manager is to make sure that people are aware of their goals. This sounds obvious, but how often are high-level strategic decisions made in the boardroom, with tasks necessary to reach the high-level goal handed down in chunks to various departments? The second major implication is that, to be motivating, a goal must be accepted by the employee. The best way to get acceptance is to involve the employee in setting the goal.

Last, the goal must be both specific and difficult enough to be motivating. "Do your best" is not a goal (it fails the specificity test). A goal that is too easy is not motivating, and an impossible goal is definitely demotivating. Part of the art of being an effective manager is identifying the fine line between setting a specific, challenging goal (one that will achieve the highest levels of employee motivation) and setting an impossible goal. Again, the key is to involve the employee in the goal setting. The employee knows best what he is capable of and will set challenging goals as long as he has not been burned by ill-conceived "management by objective" type goal-setting exercises that held him accountable for variables beyond his control. Employees who are asked to set specific, difficult goals should be given the opportunity to revisit and renegotiate the goals on a regular basis. The most demotivating use of "management by objectives" involves setting goals in January, then ignoring all of the intervening factors and other special projects and "dinging" people in December for not meeting that year's goals.

Mixing Motives

Given the wide variety of motivational theories, it is no wonder that there is widespread confusion in many organizations about the best way to design jobs and reward and recognition systems. One element that sheds some light on the issue is the differentiation between intrinsic and extrinsic motivating factors.

The basic difference between the two types of motivation is the source of the motivation. When motivation comes from external factors, such as pay or other rewards, it is called *extrinsic* motivation. When the source lies within the person such as the sense of enjoyment and satisfaction that come from doing a task, it is called *intrinsic* motivation.

Rewarding people can have an interesting effect, at least experimentally. When we reward people for doing things they previously did for pure enjoyment, they quit doing it for enjoyment. Think about the implications for reward systems in organizations. When you start getting paid for doing something you love, do you quit doing it just for the love of it?

The confusion in the answer to this question lies in the fuzzy boundaries between external and internal motivation. Suppose you give someone on your staff a $2,000 bonus for the extra work she did to ensure that a project was completed successfully. This clearly fits the definition of an extrinsic reward—a monetary reward given by the boss. Does this mean the work was not intrinsically rewarding as well? Not at all. The $2,000 is not just cold, hard cash. It symbolizes something to the employee; it makes her feel recognized and appreciated.

Do extrinsic rewards work? Yes. They generally produce the behavior at which they are targeted. Do they produce commitment, passion, and the other intangibles that cause organizations to succeed? No. To get commitment, rather than compliance, extrinsic rewards must have intrinsic value; they must increase an employee's feelings of achievement and recognition. This goal is best addressed by the job enrichment variables we have discussed, such as variety and significance.

The fuzzy boundary between intrinsic and extrinsic motivators typifies the real world, a world in which one motivating factor is not always paramount. In fact, most of the time situations can best be described as involving mixed motives. More often than not, satisfying one motive may leave others unsatisfied. Psychologists have identified four situations of mixed motivation:

1. *Approach-approach* conflicts involve situations where there are two equally attractive but mutually exclusive alternatives available to you. If you receive two good job offers, you can't take them both.

2. *Avoidance-avoidance* conflicts arise when there are two equally unattractive alternatives that you must choose between. You may really hate working on a particular project, but if you don't finish it, you are likely to be fired.

3. *Approach-avoidance* conflicts occur when one goal you are striving to achieve has both good and bad consequences. If you accept a promotion, you will get a higher

salary, more prestige, a company car, and the opportunity to do new and challenging work. However, you really enjoy your current job and will have to give up many enjoyable tasks and a tight-knit group of coworkers and move to a distant city to take the promotion.

4. *Multiple approach-avoidance* situations can really give you a headache! In this case, you are offered two options, each of which has clear advantages and clear disadvantages.

What can you do when faced with situations like these? What can you do to help your employees when they are placed in similar situations? Fortunately, people have built-in drives that motivate them to resolve such conflicts, because the cognitive dissonance they cause is uncomfortable. You need to figure out a way to tip the scales one way or another in making these decisions, and the traditional list of pros and cons is a helpful way of doing so. When there really are no clear-cut right answers, it is sometimes helpful simply to choose an alternative and not look back. Some people have tendencies toward "buyer's remorse," in which the alternative they rule out becomes much more attractive the minute they commit to a different course of action. Realizing that this will occur and refusing to give the remorse any credence will help. It is, however, a skill that often has to be fostered.

The Role of Individual Differences

The various theories of motivation assume that there is a basic human nature, that we can make generalizations about people and manage them accordingly. Fortunately for managers, this is partly true. Unfortunately, there is the obvious fact that people are different. If you supervise a fairly large number of people, the motivation theories give you some guidance on formulating policies and procedures in a way that will create a motivating environment for groups of people. The fact that there are individual differences, though, forces us to ask the question: What motivates individuals?

Some managers simply choose a course of action that they believe will motivate most of the people most of the time. That works very well the majority of the time, and that might be enough. But there may be occasions when the question of what motivates individuals may need to be answered.

If you have a "problem employee," you may find that person taking up a disproportionate amount of your time and energy. An investment in some time spent exploring this individual's motivational state may well pay off in decreased problems and headaches for you. In addition, there may be times when it is to your benefit to treat people differently. This situation is probably best addressed by the idea, from expectancy theory, that different employees will place different values on what you have to offer them.

When you wish to reward behaviors at work and your efforts backfire, the cause can often be traced to individual differences. If you have two men on your staff, one of whom is an older man with a family, nearing retirement and concerned about his nest egg, and the other a young college student, living with his parents and working for money to buy gas for his car and go on dates, they are clearly motivated by different things. Imagine that you have some work that needs to be done and offer each of these men an opportunity to work overtime. You may get two very different responses:

"Thank you! I owe you one."

"Well, if you really need me, I'll stay. But you owe me."

These differences are not surprising. But how often are we taken aback when our efforts to do something for employees backfire?

Everything we have to offer people in organizations will be valued by them to differing degrees. This includes what Herzberg called the hygiene factors as well as the motivators. It's simple: Provide for the release of motivation in each person who works for you. It's not easy. There is no way that company policies and procedures can do it. Blanket policies can only address generalizations and hope to create a motivating environment for most people. Most of the time, that ought to be sufficient. When it isn't, the art of management is required.

It ought to be clear by now that management is a situational art. The correct course of action in any case depends on the situation and is not to be found in any textbook. What are the implications in this for concerns about consistency and fairness?

There is no way that policies and procedures can substitute for managerial judgment. In many organizations, supervisors, team leaders, and other first-level managers are expected to police company policy by following the rules. Consistency, in the minds of many organizations, equates to fairness. This argument is obviously flawed. Suppose your company's policy is that anyone who uses three sick days in one month is given a letter of reprimand. Suppose you have two people on your staff who used their third day yesterday. You give both of them a letter of reprimand, right? And you dismiss as irrelevant the fact that one of them was too hung over from weekend parties to come to work and one was in the emergency room with a sick child.

Unfortunately, in most organizations the flexibility to deal with different situations differently is reserved for higher levels of management. The higher you rise in an organization, the easier it is to use policies and procedures as guidelines instead of as rulebooks. Organizations need to pay more attention to giving the first-level managers the training and the skills needed to use managerial judgment in dealing with people. Otherwise, you may motivate a large percentage of the workforce, but many more are falling through the cracks.

Productivity: The Result of Managing Motivation

Organizations demand results. Without results (however that is defined), the organization will not survive. Managing motivation is not just an attempt to make the workplace a satisfying place to be; it is also a requirement for productivity.

Productivity is the result of a lot of different factors. When the individual worker is considered, it can be described most easily as the interplay between ability and motivation. Ability (can he do the work?) is best addressed through proper hiring and training procedures. Motivation (will he do the work?) is much harder to gauge. Although many of us believe we can assess the motivation to work through, say, a job interview, it is not that easy.

The biggest problems arise when motivation and ability are confused. Any kind of incentive program, training, or hiring procedure that confuses the two is bound for failure. Ability is clearly the easier of the two to manage. Ensuring that someone can do the work is a matter of hiring people with the right amount of skill and knowledge, perhaps by asking them to demonstrate their ability, or giving people the training to do the tasks required and making sure they have the proper tools and equipment and enough time to do the job correctly. If these factors are not in place, no amount of motivation will allow the job to be done right. Imagine the frustration of an employee who is "treated" to a motivational speaker who exhorts her to do a better job, when she knows that her poor results are due to constant equipment malfunction.

Conversely, when an employee has chosen not to perform (a motivational problem), treating the situation as an ability problem is also a waste of time and money. Training department managers in organizations all over the world are used to hearing requests like "We need a sales training program!"

The savvy training manager will ask: "Why do we need sales training?"

"Because this quarter's sales are way down."

"Have you had a lot of turnover in the sales department?"

"No."

"So these are the same people whose sales figures were excellent last quarter?"

"Yes."

"So you're saying that they have forgotten how to sell?"

This is only the tip of the iceberg in what is known as needs assessment in the training field, but the idea is that there may be a variety of reasons for the dip in sales (the economy, the product, the commission structure), and sending the salespeople through sales training may or may not be the answer. In fact, what they need may be motivational in nature (e.g., better incentives or a better product to sell).

The Process Improvement Team: Part 2

Consider the example that opened this chapter. The people in the process improvement teams did not feel good about themselves because the company bought them T-shirts, pizza, or a holiday party. They felt good about themselves when they were able to accomplish something, to contribute something to the organization that was of value. This was such a powerful influence on their behavior that it brought about levels of productivity not seen from some of them in many years.

The critical lesson here is that most people want to make a difference, do meaningful work, and be recognized for it. All the other things are just what Herzberg would call hygiene factors. Those things will never elicit the motivation and productivity that the job itself can bring. Managers have been told this since Maslow's day, but many organizations have had a hard time hearing it. I have no idea why, but I personally have seen it over and over again. Instead of doing something that is cheap or free (redesigning the work to be more meaningful and arranging for recognition), managers do things that are expensive (trips, parties, prizes). The cheap/free option is more valuable to both the organization and the employee. Go figure.

What Do You Need to Know About Motivation?

Unmet needs motivate behavior. All people have a need for esteem, both self-esteem and esteem from others. For most of us, this need is not completely met; therefore, anything that makes us feel good about ourselves motivates us. This is the simplest and most overlooked tenet that could help managers become better managers.

Manager's Checklist

☐ People are driven by activity, curiosity, and manipulation. How well do the jobs you provide allow for these needs?

☐ The five levels of needs Maslow talked about are physiological or survival needs (food, water), safety needs (shelter), social needs (belongingness, love, acceptance), esteem needs (self-esteem and the esteem of other people), and self-actualization (self-development and the realization of potential). Your employees all have some unmet esteem needs, and unmet needs motivate behavior. Your employees usually have their survival and safety needs met, and met needs do not motivate behavior. Does your treatment of employees reflect this knowledge?

☐ Job enrichment involves designing jobs in such a way that the job itself is motivating. Do you do all that you can to make your employees' jobs as interesting as possible and build in some variety, some autonomy, plenty of feedback, and a sense of the significance of the task?

☐ Expectancy theory can be used to analyze the motivational level of a job as well. Are jobs rewarded by outcomes employees value, is there a perceived connection between performance and rewards, and is there a perception among employees that they can do the job?

☐ How does the mix of extrinsic and intrinsic rewards that you offer add up? Is there a good balance?

☐ Are you trying to reach everyone by being consistent, only to have your efforts backfire? Can any of the "motivational problems" you experience among your employees be explained by individual differences?

5

"It's Enough to Make You Sick"
—*Stress and Anxiety*

Stress is a fact of life in organizations today. The fast pace, the financial pressures, and the increasing demands for both quality and productivity result in an atmosphere that many people find tremendously stressful. (There are some people, of course, who find such an atmosphere invigorating and would be bored with anything less.)

What do we know about stress in organizations? What about the individual differences that lead one person to find a situation extremely stressful while another does not? And what can you do with your knowledge to manage your own stress and that of your staff?

The Merger: Part 1

You are the manager of an accounting department in a large firm that is getting ready to merge with another company. The due diligence process is going to require that your staff provide volumes of information, and the quality of the presentation may determine whether any of you will be invited to remain with the company after the merger.

At a staff meeting, you let your employees know in no uncertain terms what this project means to you and, you hope, to them. In your anxiety to turn out the best possible product, you set daily goals for them, check with them several times a day, and point out anything that requires reworking.

One Monday, two of the five people who report to you call in sick. One says that she has been fighting a migraine all weekend and is not likely to be able to come to work until midweek. The other has a bad cold and hopes to be in Tuesday.

All day Monday you are in a low-grade panic. The three remaining staff members work through breaks and lunch but don't make the kind of progress you know is required.

At 2:00 A.M. Tuesday morning, you awaken with a crippling pain in your chest that seems to be about to cut off your breathing. As sharp pains begin to radiate down your arm, you shake your spouse and request a call to 911.

Psychological Roots of Stress and Anxiety

One way to look at stress is to define it as a situation in which your needs are not being met. If you have a biological or psychological need and run up against obstacles in trying to meet it, frustration may result. You may experience conflict because you have two needs and can meet only one of them (e.g., you accept a promotion, which meets your need for achievement, but have to leave your old staff, who met your need for affiliation). Or you may feel stress as a result of pressure, originating internally or externally, to achieve certain goals or behave in certain ways.

Frustration, conflict, and pressure may all throw us into stressful situations. There are other variables at play, such as how important it is to you to meet the need, how long the frustration lasts, and how many needs you are trying to meet at once. The emotional component comes into play as well; frustration tends to cause anger, and a perception of threat or danger may cause fear or anxiety.

There are two categories of ways to manage psychological stress: We can try to meet the demands of the situation, or we can try to escape from the situation. The physiological roots of stress are well understood. The "fight or flight" syndrome, in which our bodies chemically mimic the physiological reactions of our caveman ancestors, is a common and almost inevitable reaction to stress. We have the same physiological systems as our most recent ancestors; when faced with a stressful situation, our bodies, like theirs, prepare either to attack the stressor physically or to run away quickly. Thus, adrenaline pumps into the system, heart rate and respiration increase, and blood leaves the limbs and head for the internal body cavities. The problem, of course, is that very few situations in modern organizations can be handled by either of the two responses for which our body is preparing us. So we handle the crisis by negotiating across a table, while the physiological responses create wear and tear on our bodies.

Physical and Mental Stress

In the workplace, physical stressors include such things as noise, crowded conditions, extremes of temperature (heat or cold), and harsh or insufficient lighting. Imagine an employee rushing to work at a retail store the week before Christmas. She hurries through the snow-covered parking lot, freezing. She enters the store, to be greeted by a mass of shoppers, a din of Christmas carols playing, and stifling heat caused by the crush of bodies. Now imagine an employee reporting for work that same day at the payroll department at a small private college. The students are on vacation, most of the instructors are gone, and members of a skeleton crew work quietly at their desks. These two very different physical environments are going to have very different effects on the physical and mental well-being of the two employees.

Mental stressors are a bit harder to measure but include some of the things mentioned in the previous section, such as pressure and conflict. Other work-related mental stressors are work overload, repetitive work, lack of control over work conditions, dangerous jobs, role conflict, and rapid changes in the work environment.

Work overload is clearly related to pressure and, ultimately, to burnout. The problem, of course, is that it is very difficult for a manager to decide just what constitutes too much work. Too little work is also somewhat boring and stressful, as is repetitive work. Even attempting to define the optimal level is difficult, since it differs from one person to the next.

If an employee perceives that he has no control over his job, he may experience stress. When organizations "overmanage" people in the name of control or consistency, a feeling of lack of control can result.

Dangerous jobs, such as working around high-power electrical lines, can be a source of stress. Any job that carries with it the threat of physical injury, dismemberment, dealing with criminals, or other hazardous duties is stressful not only to the employee but to her family.

Role conflict refers to the experience of having incompatible demands placed on you because of the multiple roles you take on in your life. You may be a parent who feels an obligation (and a desire) to attend your child's piano recital, as well as a top executive who has been called out of town to attend an important briefing at which a key new marketing strategy will be determined. This situation (and the hundreds of variations on it that take place every day in the workplace) usually arouses a great deal of stress. Any two roles may cause conflict. For example, if you are a first-level supervisor but also a member of the bowling league with some of your employees, your role as a member of the social group may conflict with your role as boss and cause you to be uncomfortable when you have to address performance-related problems.

Rapid change, whether it be in technologies, products, markets, or policies, can cause stress in the workplace. And what workplace today is not experiencing its share of rapid change?

We experience physical and mental reactions to stress. Think about how you feel when you are in a threatening or uncomfortable situation. You may begin to sweat, get cold hands, and feel your heart begin to race. Your muscles get tense, and you begin to feel some nausea or an upset stomach. These physical manifestations of stress do not distinguish between pleasurable and unpleasurable occasions; you may feel similar sensations when you are being fired from your job and when you are waiting for your first date.

As we said, there are reasons our bodies go through this kind of transformation. Our bodies are preparing for a physical confrontation of some kind or for fleeing the scene. Our hands and feet get cold because the blood vessels are constricting, which will be of benefit if we receive a wound. The body is preparing itself for a brief period of high activity, so the heart rate increases. Digestion slows, allowing blood to be diverted to major muscles, leading to the upset stomach.

Mental reactions to stress include feeling anxious, worrying, and imagining disasters. We humans are especially good at imagining the worst that can happen and then worrying about it.

The rest of this chapter looks at how to deal with all these symptoms by considering some ways of looking at stress and some ways of dealing with the issues.

Positive and Negative Stress

How can a first date and a job termination result in the same set of physical symptoms? Stress, while often portrayed in a negative light, is also essential for health and happiness. How can such a thing be?

If you have ever seen one of those checklists for measuring your stress level, you know that they are full of both positive (birth of a child) and negative (death of a spouse) events. An opportunity is a stressful situation, as is a demand or a threat. The last thing you want to do is create a stressfree workplace. Why? Because no work would get done!

Think about a stage actor who, after years in the business, still gets stage fright and butterflies in the stomach prior to a performance. The best actors learn to make this arousal work for them. In fact, having no stage fright whatsoever might result in a flat and uninspired performance. The workplace is similar in that there is a level of stress that is good, that is arousing, and that results in top performance. The trick, of course, is to find that optimal level. Before we talk about specific actions managers can take to begin to strike some of these balances, we need to understand that the optimal stress level is different for each person.

Individual Differences

A sensation of stress involves many different variables. A stressful situation can be described by looking at the event that triggered stress, the individual's reaction to the event, or the consequences of the event and the reaction. When we focus on the individual, the most helpful concept is that of hardiness.

Some of us are more hardy than others. This hardiness allows us to moderate the effects of stress. This is the variable that is missing when you take those stress questionnaires that ask you about events in your life. The idea is that if you total up all your points, the total will tell you how stressed you should be. Of course, it is not that simple. Some people find life itself quite stressful, while others are more able to take things in their stride.

Think about your own job. Do you have peers who have the same job title as you do? Do you think you have the same job? Chances are that you do not. We all define and handle our jobs differently, including the opportunities we see, the constraints we deal with, and the demands that we see as stressful. The same job does not result in the same stress levels for all people, nor does stress cause the same physical or psychological reactions in all people. When a crisis or a major problem occurs, do you see it as an opportunity to utilize your skills and show the world what you can do, or do you react with anger or frustration? You may even react neutrally, viewing the latest crisis as simply part of the job.

Personality differences lead to a wide variety of reactions to events. Your personality affects your perception of the event, as well as your overall tolerance level for stress. A simple factor like having a good sense of humor can mitigate some of the effects of stress, as can a tendency toward optimism.

The most famous personality distinction in stress research is that between Type A and Type B personalities. Certain personality factors are associated with Type A people, including feeling that one is in a hurry, being unable to relax, and enjoying competition and feeling a need to win. Obviously, these are not all bad traits to have. In fact, many Type A people are quite successful in organizations—right up until they have their first heart attack. Type As are much more likely to have heart attacks than are people who do not have these distinguishing characteristics (such people are called Type Bs). Their personalities predispose Type A people to heart disease even when all other variables (family history, smoking, obesity) are held constant.

Our personality types are of vital importance when it comes to one crucial aspect of dealing with stressful situations, and that is our perception of the situation. We perceive two things about a given situation: whether it is harmful or otherwise threatening in some way and whether we are going to be able to deal with it. Think about the last time you were getting a new boss. Did your thoughts run something like this: "Oh, great! Just when I was getting along so well with the old boss. They'll probably promote a real bottom-line person this time, given the trouble we've been having meeting our goals. I'm already working too much. My family's really going to be upset now, since I'll be having to work weekends. I can't stand it!" This individual is appraising negatively a situation that is at this time unknown or neutral and is appraising his ability to deal with it negatively as well. Contrast that with the following response: "Well, I'm sad to see the old boss go. It will be interesting to see who we get in replacement. Maybe I'll make a few calls and see if I can get some inside scoop on the new person; then I'll know what I'm dealing with." Notice that I do not suggest any nonspecific, unrealistic positive thinking ("Everything will be great! Everything will be wonderful!"). What works is a plan of action (to get more information) and a feeling of being in control of the situation. Most Type As hate the feeling of losing control over a situation. When you can't change the situation, change your perception of it; look at the choices you do have, and take action.

Even our physical arousal is subject to our own interpretation of our feelings. Suppose you are about to give a presentation to the CEO and her staff. Your heart rate has increased, and your palms are sweaty. You can interpret this in two ways: "I'm so scared!" or "I'm so excited!" The critical point here is that you will act differently depending on which of these two interpretations you choose.

Physical factors, such as diet, exercise, and overall health, also play a part in your ability to tolerate stressors. Salutary health habits seem to prepare the body better to absorb the ill effects of stress and serve as a buffer to some of the effects. There are also genetic predispositions to some stress-related illnesses, such as heart disease and some cancers.

Knowing that there are so many individual factors that affect our reactions to stress, it is obvious that our efforts at stress management have to take these variables into account.

Stress Management

Is the stress in your life generally physical, mental, or both? What about your stress reactions? Do you worry, get an upset stomach, or both? Although some of the things that buffer you from stress, like a sense of humor, can be worked on, it is never easy to change the habits of a lifetime. Any book, seminar, or video on stress management will have a similar message: Managing stress is simple. It is not, however, easy.

Managing stress is simple because we know that things like eating right and exercising will help your body absorb the ill effects of stress. Stress management is simple because thinking more positively and not worrying also works. Stress management is not easy, however, because these habits are difficult to establish. Establishing new habits is hard work, and no book or seminar can do it for you. So where do you start?

Techniques for managing stress generally fall into one of two categories: direct and indirect. Direct techniques involve acting directly on the situation that is stressing you and generally require action. Indirect coping mechanisms include making the physical efforts that prepare the body to absorb stress, like improving diet and getting regular exercise. Does it make a difference which you choose?

Suppose you are a physical stress reactor. You get headaches, you sweat, your stomach churns, and you feel jittery. The mental stress relief devices, such as thinking optimistically, may not be the best choice for you. Let's explore the coping devices in a little more depth.

Coping directly with a stressor requires that you confront it. Suppose you are extremely frustrated by a new boss who seems to be making unrealistic demands on you. You may engage in some problem solving, analyze the situation, and make some choices about whether to stay in the job. You can also choose to acquire skills to handle the situation better, perhaps by attending a class in assertiveness training or negotiation skills.

Since so much of stress is in our perception of it, we can also engage in changing our perception. This is not as hard as it sounds. Think about what you have control over in this situation. You cannot fire the boss. You may feel that, although you could quit, it is not really an option, since you need the job. What you have the most direct control over are your own reactions. Restructuring your perception of the situation goes beyond lying to yourself or being mindlessly positive. It means actively searching for alternative ways of responding to a situation.

Some of the more indirect methods of managing stress do not involve dealing with the situation directly. If, after analyzing the situation, you really feel that you have no options but to live with the unreasonable boss, there are steps you can take outside the situation.

One of the best ways to deal with stress is to ensure that you have a support network of family, friends, and colleagues. The presence of such a network mitigates the effects of stress. One important caveat: Having a support network requires that you give support as well! If you are constantly asking for support but not giving it, your network will get tired of the one-way nature of the exchange. If you don't have enough social support, foster in yourself the ability to give support. Practice asking, "And how are things with you? Did you get that promotion? Are you getting along any better with that annoying coworker?"

Distraction has also proven to be a fairly effective stress management technique. A movie, a novel, a video game, or another engrossing mental exercise can provide relief from worrisome thoughts. This technique does not solve the problem, of course, but it does provide a momentary distraction that might allow for a renewed enthusiasm for coping with the problem at a later time.

The purely physical stress management techniques are at the indirect end of the spectrum. Systematic relaxation, whether it is a formal meditation program or simply some quiet time alone, can help you to identify what is going on in your body. Tense muscles can be deliberately relaxed, warding off aches and pains. Anxiety can be turned off for twenty minutes or so. Again, this relaxation is difficult to do at first and must be learned. But the physical effects, in lowered blood pressure and a heightened sense of well-being, are well documented.

Last on the physical end of the continuum are the deceptively simple items, diet and exercise. These two alone are extremely powerful in reducing the effects of stress; yet how many of us have said, "Oh, I just don't have time to eat right. Exercise? I'm exhausted by my stressful job and you want me to exercise?" Carefully examine thoughts like these. If you are willing to invest some time in yourself, eat more healthy foods, and arrange for even moderate exercise, you can reduce your levels of anxiety and stress. Think about what such an investment is worth to you. Then, if you choose not to do it, recognize your free choice by stating it that way: "I choose not to eat right. I choose not to exercise."

Stress and Managers

There are stressors in life and in the workplace, there are various reactions to stress, and there are various coping mechanisms available to deal with the harmful effects of stress. It is important that you deal with your own stress and that of the people who work for you. Your payback will be more productivity, less absenteeism, and less turnover. In this section, we concentrate on managerial actions that can reduce stress, both the manager's own and the organizational stress levels.

Managers whose jobs contain a high degree of perceived stress are often unhappy and unhealthy. Short of quitting, what can you do about such jobs so that you can be mentally and physically healthier? Some managers choose to deal with the stress of their jobs by working harder or switching to a different task when they feel one task becoming stressful. These techniques are a prescription for burnout. Some of the more effective work-related techniques include delegating more or analyzing the situation and changing how the work is done.

It won't be surprising to hear that the best way to deal with a stressful managerial job is to build resistance to stress through better health habits. It takes only ten minutes to walk around the block. Fresh fruit is as easy to eat at meetings as a donut, and orange juice can be substituted for coffee. Alcohol and tobacco consumption (as well as the consumption of illegal substances) may temporarily mask the stress, but the long-term damage is a high price to pay.

Have you taken all the vacation that you are entitled to this year? Did you relax on your vacation, or did you work around the house and check your messages every hour? The ability to relax and to balance work and leisure is important for stress management. Do you foster an optimistic attitude? Keep as close an eye on your internal thoughts as you do on your sales numbers or your stock prices. Pessimistic thoughts are as self-defeating as poor health habits.

Notice your habits. Commit to changing them realistically. Don't stress yourself further by making this an obsession (spending five evenings a week at the gym is, for most people, unrealistic), but don't give up, either. If you can make one small change (walking around the block at lunch, eating an apple instead of a donut on your coffee break) every three weeks or so, you are making great progress at changing the habits of a lifetime! If you can catch yourself in one pessimistic or self-defeating thought, change the thought, and remind yourself to try being optimistic next time, optimism will eventually become a habit.

What about your role as a manager of other people? When you try some change techniques and they begin to work for you, it is tempting to become a zealot. Be careful about trying to force them on others; stress begins and ends in each person's own thoughts and beliefs. You can, however, do some specific things that will help those who work for you. First, delegate reasonably. You may relieve your own stress by dumping all your work on your subordinates, but all you are doing is passing the stress along. Give people the time, the training, and the support to help you. As we saw in Chapter 4, people like having a challenging job to do.

You can cut out the coffee and the donuts at meetings in favor of juice and fruit, but don't go so far as to forbid coffee and donuts. You can invite people to join you on a midday walk, but don't force the issue. You can substitute optimistic ways of looking at a situation when you hear people say, "Ain't it awful" and still avoid looking like an unrealistic dreamer.

What about the specific work-related stress factors that we discussed (work overload, lack of control, repetitive work, danger, role conflict, and rapid change)? Many of them are related to the way the job or the organization is structured; depending on your level in the organization, you can take direct or indirect action to change them.

Work Overload

Work overload is fairly common in some organizations and occurs at least occasionally in most organizations. Many organizations have downsized, and the remaining staff is expected to pick up the extra work. Although Total Quality Management (TQM) has lost favor as the answer to all organizational problems, it has given us many tools to deal with this issue. Continuous improvement, process improvement, and other quality concepts have given organizations the ability to work smarter and get more done with less. One of the basic premises of TQM is that there is a lot of wasted effort in organizations, such as scrap, rework, checking, and excessive paperwork. Simple process mapping techniques and continuous process improvement can not only reduce the workload but it can make employees feel as if what they are doing is important, rather than pointless paperwork or endless reworking of something that wasn't done right the first time. One of the side benefits of this approach is that it requires a cross-functional view of work, so various departments have to work together more closely. This brings the added benefits of letting the employee see the big picture and how he fits into it.

Lack of Control

Another contributor to employee stress is the feeling of having no control over one's work. Whether it is the choice of task, the pace of the work, or the specific steps to reach a goal, organizations often police and overcontrol workers in the name of consistency. The whole point behind participative management is that employees are less stressed when they feel more in control of their work lives. An added benefit is that the manager's stress can be lowered as well when daily tasks are delegated to those closest to the work. (As we have noted, we all feel the need for power. If you are hesitant to delegate or allow employee participation in decision making, take an honest look at your own need for power. If you are telling yourself things like "I can't trust anyone else with these decisions" or "They'd only screw it up," chances are you are deceiving yourself.)

Repetitive Work

The stressor that we referred to as repetitive work involves boring, narrow tasks. The problem is best addressed by job enrichment. Suppose you wish to enrich the job of a dishwasher in a restaurant. The first step in job enrichment is to ensure that the job contains a variety of tasks. This does not mean that in addition to washing the pots and pans, she gets to wash the silverware. This may mean that she is given the responsibility of ordering the cleaning supplies from the vendor.

Task identity is also important in job enrichment and involves being able to point with pride at "my job." Enriching the dishwasher's job may allow her to identify herself as the kitchen coordinator (this is not just an empty change of title but involves making her responsible for a wider range of duties). The employee must also be allowed to feel that her task is of some significance. As her manager, you may need to communicate to her the importance to the customer and to the restaurant's reputation of having the dishes clean.

A sense of autonomy is important, as well. While the dishwasher may not be able to choose what hours she works, she may be given some latitude on which tasks she tackles and in what order, as long as the overall goals of the establishment are met (the lunch- and dinner-hour clean-dish needs are met).

The last way to design jobs to reduce stress is to build in feedback mechanisms. The dishwasher may have to work very hard at times during her shift, but that is more acceptable if she knows how she is doing. Is she keeping up with the demand for clean dishes? Are people waiting while empty tables stand in need of clean silverware? We all have a strong need for feedback. It is no fun, and ultimately it is stressful, not to know how we are doing. Imagine playing golf and not knowing until the game is over how you did. You hit the ball blindly each time, and someone tells you when it's time to move on to the next hole. It would be a boring and pointless game without feedback, as would most games and most jobs.

Think of a job (yours, or that of someone who works for you). How can the five tenets of job enrichment be used to increase the satisfaction and reduce the stress of that job? Can there be more task variety built in, more identity, more significance, more autonomy, and more feedback? The answer is usually yes, and the paybacks are many and varied for the employee, the manager, and the organization.

Danger

What about the stressful job that is actually dangerous? What do you do to relieve the stress of the police officer, the twenty-four-hour convenience store graveyard-shift worker, and other jobs that involve actual physical dangers? Realistically, a person accepting such a job realizes the dangers involved. What the organization can do is make sure that the individual receives regular and ongoing safety education. The stress on the graveyard shift may be lessened if the person receives not just a memo on safety procedures but regular training and perhaps the opportunity to practice the actions to take when confronted by an armed robber. The more prepared and confident the individual feels, the less likely he will be to spend his work hours anxiety-ridden about the possibility of danger.

Role Conflict

Role conflict is a more difficult issue to address. Conflict between work and nonwork roles, such as executive and parent, can be addressed through flexible scheduling. Some companies are providing on-site day care to reduce the absenteeism caused by unreliable babysitters or lack of quality day care. Some companies allow for time off to attend parent-teacher conferences or even allow the parent paid leave to volunteer at a child's school a number of hours per year. The rate of involuntary out-of-town transfers has decreased somewhat, as companies begin to recognize the reality of the two-income family and perceive the uprooting of children that results from transfers as being less than desirable to many employees.

Work-related role conflicts are a bit harder to address through policies and procedures. The new supervisor who experiences the conflict that comes from no longer being one of the gang needs some help in making that transition. Many large organizations have supervisory development programs where such conflicts are discussed with groups of peers. Many more organizations do not have the resources to offer such training, and the new supervisor struggles alone. If you are the new supervisor's boss, you need to recognize the inevitability of some of these conflicts and coach her through it. If you are the new supervisor, you may be tempted to go from one extreme ("I am now the boss, so tremble and obey") to another ("It's just me, we can still be friends"). The point between extremes at which you land will require that fine sense of balance that typifies a good manager. What will work for you? It depends on the prior relationship you had with your staff, how you define the job, and what you need to accomplish.

What about other role conflicts within the organization? With more cross-functional teams and cross-department cooperation required, you or your employees may have mixed allegiance. If you manage the marketing department and have an employee who belongs to a team on which the manufacturing department is represented, the old antagonisms will be hard to maintain ("Those people are lazy/stupid"). Where does the true allegiance lie? And does your own need for power and your need to protect your own turf get in the way of this kind of cross-functional progress? Before you say no and move on, keep in mind that there is a lot of old-style "turfism" and territory protection going on in organizations. If everyone reading this book pleads "not guilty," who is guilty of all of this territorialism? Chances are it is you, at least to some extent. Before your defense mechanisms kick in too strongly, remember to keep an open mind to the possibility that you might be part of the problem. The good news, of course, is that you can also be part of the solution. Do your employees feel some conflict or mixed loyalties within the company? Do you demand strict allegiance to your department? There are probably at least vestiges of this old-style management within you if your employees are feeling these conflicts. The solution then starts with you as well.

Rapid Change

The last organizational fact of life that causes stress is the huge issue of change. The stress brought about by changing technologies, customer needs, and jobs, in addition to organizational changes such as mergers and acquisitions, cannot be handled by direct means. Neither you nor the people who work for you can simply stop the changes if the organization is to survive. The question then becomes: How do you help people manage the stress that change brings?

We all have a natural built-in tendency to resist change, and this resistance has developed in us for a lot of good reasons. When we feel a certain level of competence in our job, we may wish to hold on to that job because to change is to become less competent. Change is frightening, accompanied as it is by the loss of the old way. As with many of the other stress management techniques, the key to managing change is to learn to identify how you are perceiving a given situation, then actively work to change that perception.

Change usually involves a loss or a giving up of something (old ways, old machinery, old friends). We can choose to dwell on this loss, or we can identify what we are gaining from the change (new skills, new technology, new friends). There are almost always gains as well as losses; teach yourself and your staff to identify and take advantage of the positives. This will reduce victim mentality, the "woe is me," pessimistic attitude that does not have any value for the person or the organization. Fostering the active, "what do we stand to gain" approach heightens the ability to be flexible, and since change is a constant in organizations today, the sooner this flexibility is developed, the happier everyone will be.

Specific technological changes require specific training. Resistance to a new piece of machinery, for example, can be lessened by thorough training and by fostering an understanding of the machine's advantages over the old system. When possible, having true participation in the decision-making process that leads to changes can also be helpful. Be careful, though, with "lip-service" participative management. If the decision has already been made, don't ask people for their input. Oddly enough, when you ask an employee for input, he expects you to do something with the information or opinions he provides! Asking for input on a decision that has already been made is not only pointless; it is demoralizing.

In general, a supportive atmosphere helps employees deal with the stress of change. While you don't want to encourage pessimism, an atmosphere that allows employees to express their concerns is healthy. At least, when the concern is expressed, you know what it is and can provide information to counter it. An unexpressed concern leads to resistance to change that is much harder to deal with because it is unexpressed.

The Merger: Part 2

It should be obvious by now that all the physical symptoms affecting the people in the example that opened this chapter were stress-related. The migraine, the bad cold, and the chest pains were all to some extent caused or exacerbated by the situation. What could the manager have done differently?

The manager was stressed and passed the stress along to the staff. A lot of energy was expended in worry and anxiety in this example, energy that would obviously have been better spent on the task at hand. The manager needed to control his own stress level before delegating the tasks to the staff. The anxiety revealed by his overcontrol backfired, since the very goals the manager hoped to achieve (that the staff would see the importance of the task and work hard on it) were undermined by the physical toll on the staff.

Suppose the manager had chosen just one of the stress management techniques discussed in this chapter, altering perceptions. He would have had to do a lot of work in his own mind, and part of it might have gone as follows:

"What is the absolute worst thing that can happen?"

"I can lose my job."

"And what are the odds of losing your job?"

"In the last company that this company acquired, 20 percent of the managers lost their jobs."

"What would happen then, realistically?"

"Well, I'm thirty-five years old and fairly well-connected in my industry. I'd probably find another job within six months or so."

In this short mental exercise, the manager has substituted facts and research for emotion. He is now better prepared to communicate a sense of urgency to his staff, while also providing them with a good model of how to handle yourself in uncertain situations. His next step is to involve the staff in deciding how they will attack the tasks, perhaps provide some social support by taking them out to lunch together when various milestones are reached, and in the process keep both himself and the staff members out of the emergency room.

What Do You Need to Know About Stress?

While there are many kinds of stress, many possible re-actions to stressful situations, and many specific stress management techniques, there are some basic rules that will help. First and foremost, remember that you and your employees choose to perceive situations in certain ways. That perception is a powerful contributor to the stress you feel. That perception is also the variable over which you have the most control.

Manager's Checklist

☐ What physical stressors are there in the workplace(s) for which you are responsible?
  • Harsh or insufficient lighting
  • Uncomfortable temperature variations (heat or cold)
  • Crowded conditions
  • Noise

☐ What mental stressors are present?
  • Pressure
  • Conflict
  • Rapid change

☐ Teach your employees that their own personalities play a part in determining their stress levels.
  • Humor
  • Optimism
  • Their perceptions and appraisals of situations

☐ Teach your employees specific stress-management techniques.
  • Problem-solving and analysis
  • Specific job training when needed
  • Time management
  • Relaxation
  • Diet and exercise

☐ Provide a supportive environment for stress management.
  • Allow employees to provide each other with social support
  • Foster participation in decision making
  • Give employees control over their jobs whenever possible
  • Design jobs to be interesting and enjoyable
    —More task variety
    —More identity
    —More significance
    —More autonomy
    —More feedback

6

"She Is One Smart Cookie!" —*Intelligence*

Intelligence is a general characteristic of people that refers to their capacity to learn, to use information, and to interact effectively with the world. What do we know about intelligence, and how can this knowledge help you be a more effective manager?

A Top-Notch Employee: Part 1

There is a woman in your company whom you consider one of your most valuable employees. She has been in your employ for eight years, and during that time she has spent her days cleaning the offices from top to bottom. She keeps all of the restrooms clean, neat, and stocked with supplies. She cleans the cafeteria three times a day. She washes windows in the lobby, keeps the reception area picked up, and even collects litter in the parking lot. She is clearly happy at her work, cheerfully greeting most employees by name and rarely missing a day's work. She is proud of what she does, often asking you or her supervisor to take a look at something she just finished ("See how nice the lunch room looks?"). This valuable employee has an IQ of 70 and was considered unemployable prior to being given an opportunity at your company.

In this chapter, we will consider the basic concept of intelligence by exploring the following areas:

- What is intelligence?
- How do we get it?
- How is it measured?
- How does intelligence relate to success on the job?

What Is Intelligence?

Intelligence can be looked at in many ways. Researchers have described it as anything from a very general concept to a combination of more than one hundred specific abilities. For our purposes, we can take a middle ground and define intelligence as a general mental capacity that includes many specific abilities, such as the ability to reason, to comprehend, to use abstract concepts, to solve problems, and to plan.

The general factor that influences overall intelligence can be seen by looking at how abilities correlate. An excellent ability to reason, for example, usually goes hand-in-hand with an enhanced ability to solve problems. The more specificity that is included in a definition of intelligence, the more variability is built in; one specific ability, such as the ability to speak articulately, may not be correlated with another specific ability, such as the ability to work with numbers.

The overall intelligence level of a person may tell us a great deal about him, or it may tell us very little. It depends on what we need to know. If you were hiring a CEO for your company, intelligence might be one of the things you would look for. There are other qualities the successful candidate might be expected to show, but intelligence is probably needed for a such a complex job.

If you were hiring an accountant, knowledge of the applicant's general intelligence level would be far less helpful to you than specific knowledge of her numerical ability.

A theory developed by the researcher Robert Sternberg suggests that there are three different types of intelligences. The first is the traditional conception of intelligence, the rational, analytical type, which he calls componential. This involves the typical mental processes we call intelligence, such as analyzing and problem solving.

In addition to this traditional view, however, Sternberg identifies two other types of intelligence—creativity and common sense. Creativity, which he calls experiential intelligence, is the ability to combine experiences into new ways of thinking and acting. A person with experiential intelligence is flexible and adaptable and can adjust easily to new ideas and new tasks. Common sense, or contextual intelligence, involves the ability to adapt to the environment. This is a very practical type of intelligence, as its name implies.

When you are working with your staff on a project, think about how the various types of intelligence identified by Sternberg might work together. A group of people who are all high in componential intelligence will solve a problem logically and analytically but may not go beyond the facts of the matter and see the possibilities. If you are asking them to do something creative, such as develop a new marketing compaign, you may want to ensure that somewhere on the team experiential intelligence is represented. And if the project requires "street smarts," such as a plan to implement drastic changes in an employee benefit plan, look for someone who has contextual intelligence or you may fail to anticipate all of the possible employee reactions.

Sternberg's work was very helpful in suggesting the

existence of different types of intelligence, but other re-searchers went well beyond his three types. A Harvard psychologist, Harold Gardner, also questioned the idea that intelligence is only one quality. He outlined seven different kinds of intelligences, or talents, that make it easier for people to learn certain skills: linguistic, logical-mathematical, spatial, musical, bodily-kinesthetic, inter-personal, and intrapersonal.

Linguistic intelligence refers to a general talent for language. A linguistically intelligent person has an ear for the nice turn of phrase, notices mistakes in grammar and word use, and learns best when able to read or hear the lesson. Linguistic intelligence is probably closely linked to success in school, considering the fact that lec-tures, tests, and papers all require an adeptness with words. Many standardized tests are more closely corre-lated with verbal ability than with any other factor.

Logical-mathematical intelligence is the second clearly distinct type of intelligence. Having this type of intelligence makes an individual good at conceptual thinking, reasoning, and organization. Such an individ-ual is good at logic problems and computers.

Spatial intelligence refers to having an eye for form and visualization. A spatially intelligent person is able to find his way around a new city quickly, can draw and design things accurately, and can do jigsaw puzzles quickly.

Musical intelligence is the fourth domain. The musi-cally intelligent person is tuned in to the auditory world around her. Not only does she like music and perform-ers; she is aware of and enjoys all types of sounds in the world around her.

A fifth type of intelligence is known as bodily-kinesthetic. A person having this type of intelligence is tuned into his own body and is alert to data received through body sensations. He tends to communicate through gestures, needs to move to learn, is a good dancer, and can work well with his hands.

Interpersonal intelligence is intelligence about other people. An individual with interpersonal intelligence is emphathetic and aware of other people's feelings and reactions and tends to be sociable.

Intrapersonal intelligence refers to the ability to know oneself. The person who has intrapersonal intelligence is self-aware. She is tuned in to her own thoughts, feelings, and emotions. This type of intelligence is the subject of a 1995 book by Daniel Goleman called *Emotional Intelligence.* Goleman talks about self-awareness and emotional control, persistence, self-motivation, and social deftness. His research shows that people of traditional intelligence (high IQ) may not do as well in life as people with emotional intelligence. Goleman believes that the forces shaping today's workplace call for an increasing amount of emotional intelligence because it is the foundation for handling frustration, cooperating with other people, and resolving conflicts.

The idea of emotional intelligence was further explained by a Yale psychologist, Peter Salovey, who suggests that emotional intelligence has five segments: knowing one's emotions, managing emotions, being self-motivated, recognizing emotions in others, and handling relationships.

Being tuned in to your emotions gives you the ability to recognize them without being a slave to them. People without this ability feel helpless in the face of anger, frustration, or fear; they are carried away by the emotion of the moment. Being aware of emotion allows you to monitor it: "I am too angry to talk about this right now."

Once you recognize your emotions, you are capable of the next step, which is managing them. This emotional self-control is essential for self-motivation, which usually means that your impulses are under control and you are able to delay gratification of your impulses in the service of a greater goal.

Recognizing emotions in other people is a first step toward having good relationships with other people. Feeling empathy and being tuned in to other people lay the groundwork for cooperation and interpersonal effectiveness in general.

The ability to know oneself in these ways is one of the most critical abilities for an effective manager to have. If you can step outside yourself, observe the effect of your feelings and actions on other people, and analyze your own emotions, you have taken the first step toward being able to control or at least adapt your behavior. Many managers who self-destruct do so because they either seem blind to the implications of their actions or become carried away by their feelings. Think about this as it applies to yourself. If this whole concept makes you a little impatient, it may be a signal to you that a little bit of introspection may be helpful to you. Be aware, however, that if you are not in the habit of introspecting, it will be very difficult to do. Be patient with yourself, and enlist the help of some trusted people around you to get a true handle on your behavior.

What about applying all of this to those who work for us? How do all of these types of intelligences help us manage people in the workplace? Imagine that you are having a staff meeting. You have a capable and hardworking group, all of whom are good at what they do. In fact, they have probably gravitated to the jobs they have because of their innate talents.

The hypothetical staff meeting includes the director of finance (logical-mathematical and musical), the director of human resources (interpersonal and kinesthetic), and the director of public relations (linguistic and spatial).

As you begin the meeting, the public relations person is listening intently, taking notes, and making rapid sketches of ideas that occur to him as you describe the situation. The finance person is also listening but is not taking notes and does not appear too intent on the details. The human resources person is moving things around on the table and playing with a pen; she interrupts you to say, "You look a little stressed. Are you getting a cold?"

When you finish your speech about the budget cuts that need to be undertaken immediately in your division, you get the following responses:

"I'll run the numbers right away and see what the total percentage of cuts will look like."

"I'll begin drafting a memo to all employees that spells out the situation."

"I'll talk to some people and see what the mood on the street is."

You can guess which person made each of these statements. The point is that you need all of these points of view on your staff. What intelligences are your strong points? If you have a preference for, say, linguistic intelligence, you will enjoy working with people who are like you. What you need, though, is people unlike you to complement your style. Are all of the intelligences represented on your staff? Are you able to recognize the varied contributions each makes? If you find yourself annoyed at someone ("Quit fidgeting and pay attention" or "Why don't you ever appear to take these things seriously?"), that may be your cue that the person is approaching the situation from a different perspective than you are, and it is a perspective that may help to round out your own approach to the situation.

How Do We Develop Intelligence?

The development of intelligence can be looked at from at least two perspectives: its development in the human

species and its development in individual human beings.

Human Intelligence

The development of intelligence in our species can best
be described by looking at the development of the brain.
The oldest part of our brains, in evolutionary terms, is
the lowest part, closest to the spinal cord. This part of
the brain is very similar to the brain of a reptile. Much
of what we refer to as instinctive behavior has its roots
here.

The next part to evolve was the part of the brain
known as the limbic system. This system is found in
mammals and is closely related to emotional behavior.
The limbic system monitors our sensory input and thus
affects perception and behavior. Being in the grips of a
strong emotion (joy, sadness, anger) will affect our perception of a situation and our ability to apply logical,
"intelligent" responses.

The part of the brain that developed in primates and
humans is the topmost part of our brain, the neocortex.
This is where mental activity takes place, affecting our
performance at school and at work. The trouble with
logical, rational arguments and education geared to the
neocortex is that they ignore the emotional backdrop to
intelligence provided by the limbic system.

It is important to distinguish between the right and
the left hemispheres of the brain. Much like being right-
or left-handed, we also have a preference for utilizing
one side of the brain. As with handedness, this means
not that we use only one side but simply that one side is
more or less dominant.

The right brain sees the whole; the left analyzes the
parts. The right brain uses pictures, and the left uses
words. The right brain sees the big picture and considers

all elements of a problem simultaneously; the left looks at details and considers them in sequence. Like differences in personality or perception, there is no right or wrong to being right- or left-brained. Nonetheless, it behooves a manager to be aware of her preferred style and to know that she will benefit by asking people of the opposite preference to give input on a problem, task, or project.

Is your brain and therefore your intelligence fixed after a certain age? We sometimes think that once we reach adulthood, that's the level we will always be at: "I'm not good with numbers." The fact is that we can continue to grow and develop. Animal (mostly rat) studies show actual brain changes as a result of the provision of new stimuli in what is called an "enriched environment" that includes toys, treadmills, and the like. For people, an enriched environment may mean new ideas, new books, new friends, or new experiences. To stimulate your brain, develop your own "enriched environment." Actively seek out new and different stimuli to develop the parts of your brain and the types of intelligence that you have had fewer opportunities to develop until now.

Individual Intelligence

The development of individual intelligence has been best described by Jean Piaget, a Swiss developmental psychologist. According to Piaget, our intelligence develops in four stages and by using two processes, assimilation and accommodation. *Assimilation* is the means by which we incorporate new stimuli into our existing view of the world. It is a way of using old ideas to meet new situations. If you hire someone who is blind, for example, you may decide to treat her just like your other employees. You are attempting to assimilate her into your current style of managing. *Accommodation,* on the other hand, refers to the process of changing your view of the world when the new stimulus does not fit and changing old ideas to meet new situations. With the blind employee, for example, you may come up against situations in which your old style of managing just doesn't work and that call for accommodation instead.

The four stages of mental development that, according to Piaget, take us to our adult levels of intelligence are:

1. *The sensory-motor stage.* Up to the age of about two, we learn largely through interactions with the world around us. Through our senses (seeing, hearing, tasting) and our actions (picking things up, putting them in our mouths), we learn to know the world.

2. *The preoperational stage.* From the age of two until about seven, we develop the ability to use symbols. The best example of this is language; we learn that the word *cat* refers to the fuzzy, four-footed creature that we live with.

3. *The concrete operations stage.* From age seven until about eleven, we develop the ability to use concepts, categories, and rules. We begin to realize that not all fuzzy, four-footed creatures are cats; some are dogs. This stage is called "concrete" because we are learning to reason about things we can see and feel.

4. *The formal operations stage.* Beginning at about age eleven, we begin to be able to reason not only about concrete objects or events but about abstractions. For the first time, we can deal with possibilities and hypothetical situations.

You and the other people in your organization have gone through all four of these stages. You will continue to use assimilation and accommodation throughout your life; the key for the manager is to distinguish between them in terms of their appropriate use. If you or your staff overuse assimilation, for example, you may try too hard to fit new data into what you already know. Sometimes new data call for a change of orientation or a change in your whole approach. On the other hand, if you overuse accommodation, you may change policies, procedures, and approaches too often, leading to confusion and chaos.

Be aware of these two basic ways to handle new information. Observe how you and your staff use them, and strengthen the one you use less often. Once you develop a preference, you may use a technique inappropriately simply because you are accustomed to using that style.

How Is Intelligence Measured?

Intelligence can be measured; in fact, measurement has been an area of great interest to researchers from the beginning of the history of psychological measurement. The French psychologist Alfred Binet produced a test in 1905 that measured abilities such as judgment, comprehension, and reasoning. His test was revised and modernized at Stanford University and is known as the Stanford-Binet. It was in 1916, at Stanford, that the term IQ (intelligence quotient) was first used to describe the ratio of an individual's mental age to his chronological age. A direct descendant of the Stanford-Binet is the popular series developed by David Wechsler, known as the WAIS-R (Wechsler Adult Intelligence Scale, Revised) and the WISC-R (Wechsler Intelligence Scale for Children, Revised).

An IQ score is, first of all, a measure of aptitude,

not of achievement. Although no test can measure pure innate potential, IQ tests are less dependent on specific classroom learning than are achievement tests. An IQ score is also, as we said, a ratio. The 1916 Stanford studies defined the IQ score as an individual's mental age divided by his chronological age and multiplied by 100. For example, a fifteen-year-old with a mental age of ten would have an IQ of 66; a twenty-year-old with a mental age of twenty would have an IQ of 100. An "average" person, whose mental age matches her chronological age, has an IQ of 100.

There is a great deal of debate about the validity of IQ measures and the meaning of the numbers. IQ tests have been criticized as being narrowly focused, culturally biased, and more tests of verbal ability than of anything else. In addition, some people believe that what IQ tests really measure is the ability to take tests. There is no question that a high IQ score (whatever it measures) does tend to be correlated with success in life. People with high IQ scores tend to do better in school, and therefore they stay in school in greater numbers. They also tend to pursue their education beyond high school and are more successful in college. To the extent that this sequence of events takes place, high-IQ people are better positioned to enjoy good jobs and higher income levels and all the other benefits that come with them.

In December 1994, *The Wall Street Journal* published a position paper on the topic signed by fifty-two university professors, all experts in intelligence or in closely related fields. The article defined intelligence as a general mental capability, much as we have been discussing it here. According to the article, intelligence, defined this way, can be measured, and intelligence tests do a good job of measuring it. Intelligence tests, while quite accurate, do not measure creativity, personality, character, or the myriad other factors that cause individuals to differ in their effectiveness in life and on the job. A high IQ tends to be an advantage in life, although the advantage increases as the situation becomes more complex; in situations requiring only routine decision making or simple problem solving, a high IQ does not give one an advantage. The authors also draw on research that attempted to show whether IQ is something we're born with or something that is largely a product of our environment. Research results are quite varied, but overall the results suggest that we inherit from 40 to 80 percent of our IQ. Remember, however, the brain research that showed the importance of enriched environments. The traditional debate between nature (genetic inheritance) and nurture (environment) seems to be no debate at all; both are very important.

How Does Intelligence Relate to Success on the Job?

While IQ has been shown to be strongly related to academic success, there are far fewer data to show that it correlates with success on the job. If we define *success* as a general degree of ability, satisfaction, and productivity, how do these factors relate to intelligence?

The best answer may be that there is a fit between any given individual and any given job. A poor fit may result in dissatisfaction, low motivation, and low ability to meet job requirements. A good fit may increase satisfaction, motivation, and ability. So why can't we just do away with job interviews, resumés, and so on and just pick people with the right level of intelligence for a job?

The answer, of course, is that there are many other variables at work. First of all, how do we measure success on the job? Do you ask an individual's supervisor?

Do you give her some kind of job knowledge test? Do you measure her output? All of these measures are somewhat unreliable.

A great deal of research supports the idea that the precursor of job satisfaction is the ability to do the job well. In other words, if you place someone in a job that she can do well, she will be happy and more productive. Again we come back to the concept of fit.

The implications of general intelligence level are plain. If a job is routine or repetitive, high intelligence can be a drawback. If a job is complex, low intelligence can be a liability. The implications of the specific intelligences are clear, as well. Someone who is low in interpersonal intelligence, for example, may be miserable in a human resources department because he is simply not good at dealing with people issues. The same individual may be high in logical and mathematical intelligence and would be happier and more productive in the finance department.

Intelligence and Gender

Are men and women different in the kinds of skills they bring to the workplace? Although we might be tempted to believe that they are, recent evidence does not support a difference.

Research on grade-school-age children has purported to show that girls have greater verbal ability, while boys excel in visual, spatial, and mathematical ability. This conclusion was widely reported and believed, but scientists reviewing the study concluded that the differences, even in the original research, were quite small and essentially added up to no real difference at all.

Men and women usually have different levels of physical ability, since the average man is taller and heavier than the average woman. When it comes to intelligence, however, the averages just don't fall out that easily. Even the differences in the way people think (e.g., logically or emotionally) do not clearly fall out along gender lines. A manager would be wise not to make any assumptions about ability or preference at work on the basis of gender alone.

Intelligence and Creativity

Some jobs require a particular type of intelligence known as creativity. In fact, whether creativity is part of intelligence is still debated. The traditional, analytical definition of intelligence does not include creativity, which is defined as the ability to expand on the facts at hand. Another name for creativity "divergent thinking"; thus refers to the ability to see numerous possibilities instead of always searching for the one right answer. Creative people are often perceived as being more intelligent, simply because they see things differently from those who are less creative.

Creativity can be defined as the ability to generate ideas and to see options when faced with a challenge. Creativity can lead to innovation when an idea is applied to change a procedure or a policy. The benefits for organizations in recognizing and fostering creativity are many; decisions may be better, problems may be solved more effectively, and new products or services may be devised that can be marketed. In work environments that foster creative abilities, productivity and job satisfaction may increase.

Creativity is related to right-brain activity and also to personality. Unfortunately, creative people are sometimes at a disadvantage. In school, for example, most of us were taught under a system that assumed that there was one right answer; critical thinking was discouraged, and innovative, creative answers were considered wrong. Some of this thinking has spilled over into our workplaces. Unfortunately, logic and rationality are only part of the picture, as should be evident by now.

A Top-Notch Employee: Part 2

Looking again at the example that opened this chapter, you can see that simply knowing whether someone is "smart" or not is not very helpful in assessing her value to your organization.

General intelligence levels predict success in school but have a very weak relationship to success on the job. The assessment of specific abilities is much more helpful when attempting to place someone within an organization.

If an individual's abilities and skills are used in a way that makes him feel challenged and competent, that person will tend to be more productive and satisfied and may stay with your company in a mutually beneficial relationship for a longer time than someone who did not represent as good a "fit."

What Do You Need to Know About Intelligence?

Intelligence is a general characteristic of people. It is one of many factors to consider when making decisions in the workplace. Sometimes the best person for the job is not the most intelligent candidate but the one who best fits the requirements of the job.

Intelligence is best utilized if it is not thought of as one piece of data (e.g., an IQ score). It is a dynamic characteristic, and in fact we can continue to learn and develop our various intelligences throughout our lives.

Manager's Checklist

☐ Think about the people who report to you. Can you identify linguistic, logical-mathematical, spatial, musical, bodily-kinesthetic, interpersonal, and intrapersonal intelligences in the group members (including yourself)? What types of intelligences are missing, and how can you make sure that the perspective that is missing isn't adversely affecting the decisions you make?

☐ Do you understand the importance of assimilation and accommodation in learning new things? Can you see where each might be appropriate at different times?

☐ Think about the fit between individuals and jobs in your organization. Do you have employees who are over- or underqualified for a given job? A poor fit may result in dissatisfaction, low motivation, and low ability to meet job requirements; a good fit may increase satisfaction, motivation, and ability. Most important, this holds true whether the poor fit is the result of too much or too little of a particular kind of intelligence.

☐ Is it acceptable to be creative in your work group? Are off-the-wall ideas seen as adding life to a discussion or as annoyances? What can you do to spark more creativity in yourself and in your work group?

7

"Can't We All Just Get Along?"
—Social Psychology

Once you have a fairly good handle on why people do what they do, another variable kicks in that muddies the waters considerably. That variable is the fact that group behavior differs considerably from individual behavior. When two or more people get together, a whole new set of factors begins to complicate a manager's job.

Like individual behavior, group behavior is governed by some basic tenets that are very helpful for a manager to know. As with individual behavior, sometimes the basic tenets help, and sometimes they do not. In this chapter, we take a look at some of the things we know about what happens when two or more people come together, apply them to the workplace, and give you a few more tools for becoming a more effective manager.

The Best Team Possible: Part 1

When your company won a contract for a very lucrative new project, you knew you had to put together the best team possible. The four people you chose represented a good cross-section of the knowledge, skills, and abilities needed to take the project from start to finish. Since you had only a sixty-day time frame, you relieved the team members of all other duties and turned the project over to them.

Two weeks into the sixty days, you dropped in at one of their team meetings and were distressed to find that very little had been accomplished. You reiterated the goals and objectives of the project, reminded them of the time limits, and got nothing but stony silence in return. Over the next two days, you talked to each of the four team members individually. Here is a sampling of what you heard:

Jill: I'm sick of Bob and Mark fighting all the time. Every meeting we have turns into a clash of their egos. If Bob says it's Tuesday, Mark will go look at a calendar. I thought they were going to come to blows at one meeting last week.

Bob: I never liked Adam. I knew from the day he joined the company that he was weak and had little to offer. Why don't you remove him from the team?

Mark: These people need to realize that I am the senior person on this team and give me a little respect. Can't you announce that you are appointing me team leader?

Adam: There's really no problem with the team. Jill gets upset when tempers flare, but that's bound to happen with the stressful schedule we have to follow. Women are like that, though, and she just needs to toughen up.

Many of the basic areas of interest in social psychology are represented in this brief example. In this chapter, we look at some of those areas: aggression, attitudes, attributions, conformity, cooperation and competition, impressions, and prejudice and discrimination.

Aggression

Concern about violence in the workplace has escalated in recent years, and for good reason. As we begin to look at the concept of aggression, we will find a great deal of research that can give us some clues as to how to deal with it in the workplace. In this section, we look at some causes of aggression and some suggestions for its prevention and control.

At one time, social psychologists believed that there were two basic causes of aggression—personal factors and situational factors. Many years of research have provided more evidence to support situational causes than personal. This is good news, since situations can generally be changed more easily than people can. While we all know people who seem to have a hotter temper, a shorter fuse, and in general a more aggressive personality than other people, personality has not been shown to be a perfect predictor of aggression. Other personal factors, such as gender, have also been studied at length, with mixed results.

There is more evidence for direct ties between situational factors and aggression. (Do not expect clear answers, however. Behavioral science research results are filled with "maybe" and "sometimes." We will try to pick out the gems from the huge body of research, the gems that will provide you with tools for effective management.) It is helpful to look first at five situational factors that arouse aggression; we then offer some tips on how to deal with aggression once it has been aroused.

The five situational factors that have been studied in depth are: frustration, provocation, exposure, arousal, and environmental factors.

1. *Frustration.* "Frustration leads to aggression." Everyone who has ever taken Psychology 101 is nodding

at this point. Change the old saying to "Frustration sometimes leads to aggression" and you would be closer to the truth. Frustration, which occurs when a person is blocked from attaining a goal, can range from a fleeting feeling of exasperation to a violent explosion of temper. Some people seem to have a lower tolerance for frustration than others. You begin to see why research in this area will never be able to produce black-and-white results. Frustration, at times, leads to aggression. Other times, or with other people, the same frustrating experience may lead to depression, apathy, or increased effort.

2. *Provocation.* Provocation has somewhat closer ties to aggression. If a person considers another person's actions to be provocative, he may react aggressively. The key here is perception (see Chapter 3); the action needs to be *seen* as provoking. As a manager, you may learn not to provoke certain people. You may also learn to coach your work group on ways to avoid provoking one another. You also, of course, learn that what each person considers provoking is different! What a reasonable person may consider provoking may not provide a good rule of thumb for the person you might describe as "touchy" or "thin-skinned."

3. *Exposure.* Exposure means seeing other people take aggressive action (as on television, in the movies, or at a boxing match.) The idea is that exposure to people who are behaving aggressively lowers some people's inhibitions about acting in a similar fashion. It will not surprise you at this point to hear that the evidence is mixed, especially if you have followed the arguments about exposing children to violence on television. The stance to take as an enlightened manager is somewhere between the "ban violence on television" activists (who may quote only the studies that support their position) and the people who believe the violence around us does

not affect us at all. In fact, in many issues such as this one, extreme positions on either side are the only ones that are almost always wrong!

4. *Emotional and physical arousal.* If you are aroused (by a roller coaster ride, a romance novel, a close call on the highway on the way to work), you may be more inclined to react aggressively to someone or something that annoys you. Note that the arousal can be either positive or negative. Somehow the physiological arousal increases our "readiness" for aggression.

5. *Environmental factors.* Research on environmental factors that can lead to aggression has included studies on heat, crowding, and noise. (Describes quite a few workplaces, doesn't it? Not to mention Disney World in August.) This is one of those elements for which there is more than one reason to pay attention. Remember, some of these same factors showed up as being stress-related (see Chapter 5). If you can positively affect the environment within which employees work, it will benefit them as well as you if it cuts down on aggressive tendencies.

Once aggression has been aroused by one or more of these situational factors, what's a manager to do? There are four guidelines in dealing with aggression:

1. *Don't reinforce it!* Remember when we talked about learning theory and behavior (see Chapter 2) and how behavior that is rewarded (reinforced) increases? Many people who act aggressively on a regular basis at work are doing so because the behavior works for them. If you have an employee who acts aggressively, observe the consequences. There are quite a few rewards she might be getting from the aggressive behavior. Does she get out of doing a task? Get rid of annoying people? Feel powerful because people "won't mess with me"? Changing the consequences may change the behavior.

2. *Punish it.* As we also saw in Chapter 2, punishment is a way of making an undesired behavior cease. In this context, it is probably not the best choice (but may be a choice of last resort). To be effective, punishment must follow the behavior immediately, be very aversive, and follow the behavior each and every time. We don't often have the ability to deliver punishment this efficiently. Punishment also can lead to a lot of undesirable side effects, including defensiveness, anger, sabotage, and further aggression. (While we are on the subject of what doesn't work, the idea of catharsis—working the aggression out on something else—is an approach that is not recommended. There is some doubt as to whether it works and a great deal of evidence against it.)

3. *Arrange for training in social skills.* Seminars in "anger management" have become popular among judges sentencing convicted aggressors, but they have their place in the workplace as well. Learning alternative communication skills can be very effective.

4. *Arouse an incompatible response.* There is evidence that arousing empathy, humor, or some other response that is incompatible with aggression can be very effective. When two people are in a tense, face-to-face confrontation, a (careful) use of humor can defuse the situation. By "careful" I mean that this may not be the time to make a humorous remark about the people in the dispute. Self-deprecating or neutral humor, however, can work very well. It can also work when managing your own aggression. Knowing that aggression has a hard time coexisting with empathy or joy, call up one of these emotions when you find yourself reacting in an aggressive fashion. You may want to think of all the reasons you feel sorry for the person you feel like aggressing against, for example, or think warmly of your own spouse and how glad you are that he or she is not like this person.

Attitudes

If you've ever been told that you have a bad attitude, or if you've tried to talk to someone on your staff about her attitude, you know how gray an area this is. There are few conversations more unproductive than the one that starts:

"You have a bad attitude."

"I do not!"

Part of the problem, of course, lies in the lack of specificity. You may find it more helpful not to make reference to attitudes at all but simply to tell people what you observed them do or heard them say that was unacceptable. Any reference to attitude involves speculation on your part. But since discussion about attitudes does play a part in organizational life (some organizations still rate "attitude" on the annual performance review), let's look at some of the things we do know about it.

An attitude is an evaluative reaction to a person, group, or issue. It is a relatively stable feeling about a particular event. (The fact that it is a "feeling" instead of a "thought" is what distinguishes it from a belief.) Attitudes are formed in two ways: through social learning (where we acquire attitudes from other people) and through direct experience. Attitudes developed through direct experience tend to be held more strongly and confidently than those developed through social learning.

How are attitudes altered or changed? That is the question with which managers are most concerned. If only we could change people's attitudes—toward work, toward each other, toward the boss—how very effective we could be! Looking at our definition of attitude, however, you can see that one thing that defines attitude is that it is "relatively stable." In other words, it is not easy to change. You can change a person's behavior by forcing him to do something, but you have hardly changed his attitude. According to social psychologists, two categories of actions are designed to change people's attitudes—persuasion and cognitive dissonance.

Persuasion involves direct communication that attempts to change someone's mind about something. Like all communication, it presents numerous opportunities for misunderstanding. The basic communication model requires the presence of a sender, a message, and a receiver.

Suppose that you (the boss) are trying to persuade me (the employee) to change my attitude toward something. Before you even begin talking, there are certain variables that are going to affect what I hear and how I hear you. Do I like you? I will be more open to considering what you are saying if I feel some degree of liking for you. Are you credible? Have you misled or lied to me in the past? One of the best tools managers possess is their credibility, which is very easily lost or damaged. If you misled an employee ten years ago, she will remember the incident in vivid detail. It is vital that you tend to relationships in general long before you need to call on the strength of the relationship to meet your goals.

What about the communication itself? Is it written, oral, nonverbal? Is it formal or informal? Is it repeated? All of these factors affect the persuasiveness of a message. Which way(s) is best? The answer, of course, is, "That depends." Various message formats are more or less effective under different circumstances. Ask yourself what it is you are trying to communicate and what seems the most appropriate medium. For persuasive messages, repetition is very important. You may want to deliver the message in a variety of ways while you are repeating it.

After considering the sender and the message, give some thought to the receiver. Are you talking to a skeptic or an idealist? Are you talking to someone who has some "hot buttons" you can push? Is he or she a patriot, a devoted parent, an environmentalist, an avid bowler? Tying your message to something the person already feels strongly about can increase the odds that the person will at least listen to you. If you are delivering a persuasive message to a group (your staff, perhaps), anticipate some of the objections or reactions. You know these people. You know that Joe always has an immediate negative response, that George will enthusiastically support anything you say, that Maria will be quiet in the meeting and then undermine you in the later lunchroom conversations. Anticipate and plan for these reactions.

Once you have taken the characteristics of the sender, the message, and the receiver into account and delivered your message, what are the odds that you will actually persuade people to change their attitudes? It will not surprise you to hear, once more, that there are no sure things. You may persuade some people to change or alter their attitudes, even if you don't carefully plan your communication, or you may plan perfectly and not persuade a single person to change one bit.

The second way to alter or change people's attitudes is to arouse *cognitive dissonance*. Simply put, you can get people to say or do something that is inconsistent with their attitude. They then experience cognitive dissonance, which is an uncomfortable state of affairs in which they hold two conflicting thoughts or cognitions. ("I hate the new benefits plan. I just helped my boss plan a meeting to communicate the positive aspects of the plan to all employees.") When we experience cognitive dissonance, we are motivated to change one of the thoughts and reduce the dissonance. The person in the example can change one of the two thoughts ("The new benefits plan is not so bad" or "I don't believe any of the stuff I just helped my boss develop"). If your goal is to change the employee's mind about the benefits plan, you may be able to do so by getting her to participate in something that exposes her to conflicting thoughts. Be very careful, however, not to tie such participation to either large rewards or coercion. Obviously, there is no dissonance in the thought "I hate the new benefits plan. I only helped prepare the meeting because the boss said I could have the rest of the day off/said I'd be fired if I didn't help."

Think back to the discussion in Chapter 2 on learning and the theories of conditioned responses. A negative attitude toward something can be a conditioned response. Suppose, for example, that an employee has, on two occasions, felt ill all afternoon after eating lunch in the company cafeteria ("I hate the cafeteria food because it makes me sick"). He has avoided the cafeteria food since then, and there has been no opportunity to change his attitude. If, after six months or so, his aversion has abated to the point where he will try the cafeteria one more time, and he feels ill again, the negative attitude will be strengthened considerably. If, however, he has a positive experience, and it is repeated two or three more times, his negative attitude will be considerably lessened. (The dissonance here is: "I hate the cafeteria food because it makes me sick. I ate there twice this week and did not get sick.") Instead of direct persuasion, which is an "iffy" proposition at best, consider using some form of dissonance or counterconditioning by pairing the person's negative attitude with a positive experience.

As a manager, your job often is to change attitudes by direct persuasion. When that doesn't work, you redouble your efforts. You may be undermining your own efforts, because research shows that successful persuasion can't use techniques that are extremely obvious or that make it appear that you are trying too hard. A useful alternative is to arouse dissonance, and many managers would benefit from understanding and judicious use of this technique.

All this talk of changing attitudes, of course, is brought up short by one question: Do attitudes determine behavior? If they don't, should a manager really care about attitudes? Maybe observable, measurable, work-related behavior is all a manager should worry about.

Actually, there are some links between attitudes and behaviors. Sometimes, of course, people act inconsistently. Attitudes can affect behavior very powerfully, depending on the situation. In addition, attitudes may affect behavior to a greater or lesser degree, depending on three factors:

1. How strongly the attitude is held ("I really hate the new benefits plan" versus "I'm not crazy about the new benefits plan")

2. How specific the attitude is ("I hate the new benefits plan" versus "I hate the provisions in sections 2, 5, and 7 of the new benefits plan")

3. How relevant the attitude is to the person ("I hate the new benefit plan, and it is directly affecting me and my family" versus "I hate the new benefits plan, but I'm covered by my spouse's insurance anyway so I don't use this company's")

If an individual holds an attitude that is strong, specific and relevant, you may be better off working on changing her behavior than trying to change her attitude.

Attributions

The concept of attribution involves speculating about the causes of other people's behavior. We like to be able to make sense out of what we observe so that we know how to react to it. The sequence of events goes something like this: There is an event of some kind (a behavior on the part of another person); we attribute the behavior to some cause or other; we decide on the meaning of the event; and then we have some kind of reaction to the event. Note that the "real" reason is not what causes our reaction; it is our attribution.

We like to know what lies behind people's actions so that we can predict and attempt to control what happens in the future. If Jane reacts violently to an order to clean the restroom, for example, her manager can make an attribution that relates to internal causes ("Jane gets mad easily") or one that relates to external causes ("The restroom is really disgusting right now"). Clearly, different attributions lead to very different reactions on the manager's part. "If Jane gets mad this easily, then she probably has a problem with authority and will get mad every time I tell her to do anything" is one way of reacting. "Jane cleaned the restroom the past two days; maybe it is someone else's turn" is quite a different way.

Attribution theory looks at the guidelines that people use when analyzing other people's behavior. A basic distinction is made between internal and external explanations, as in the example about Jane. Internal causes are factors like personality or ability. External causes include luck and the vagaries of the situation.

The effective manager will keep in mind two things about attributions. First is something social psychologists call the fundamental attribution error. We fallible human beings (yes, even you) make a very predictable error when we speculate about the causes of other people's behavior. We tend to attribute things to internal causes, such as personal qualities, much more often than we should, while downplaying the importance of the situational factors. The second factor is that we make the opposite error when it comes to ourselves! Win or lose, we have a tendency to attribute our successes and failures to external causes.

Think for a moment about the implications of the fundamental attribution error for processes like annual performance reviews. If we are more likely to see internal causes for behavior, we are likely to give more credit than is due for someone's successes. We are also likely to assign more blame than is appropriate for someone's failure. External factors, such as luck, are rarely considered on performance evaluations; you may be seen as mean-spirited if you say someone was just lucky or as soft if you excuse someone from accountability due to circumstances beyond his or her control. We also tend to value effort over ability. Watch the tendency to give people more credit than they deserve simply because they appeared to try harder.

What can you do about the fundamental attribution error? Not a lot, probably. It is a fairly stable human characteristic. You can, however, be aware of its influence on you and on the people around you. When you see an action ("He left papers all over the desk"), watch the tendency to turn that into a personality trait ("He's a slob"). Situational factors are important, and you will tend to underestimate them. Conversely, positive actions ("She bought me a box of chocolates again") may be an attempt to mislead us ("She is brown-nosing the boss") or may be just what they seem ("She is a nice and thoughtful person"). The lesson here may be not to jump to any judgment too quickly and to keep in mind that we are likely to underestimate the external causes of behavior.

Conformity

The concept of conformity, as used by social psychologists, has to do with people's tendency to change their behavior in order to follow some kind of accepted standard, or norm. Norms are not company policy, procedures, rules, or what people say they do. Norms are very powerful, usually unspoken, standards that determine "how we do things around here." Norms create very powerful pressures to conform.

Conformity is different from compliance, which is a change in behavior in response to a direct request. It is also different from obedience, which is a change in behavior in response to a direct command. Compliance and obedience are more overt than conformity.

Conformity can be extremely useful in an organization. It can also, of course, be very destructive. As a manager, you can either be buffeted helplessly by the vagaries of conformity or you can use it to your advantage.

First, give some thought to what the norms are in your organization or department. Remember, you will not find out by looking in a handbook or even asking people. You may have a hard time identifying the norms because you are a part of them and because they are by nature unspoken. You can begin by observing carefully "how we do things around here."

Your policy may be that people in your office work 8:00 A.M. to 5:00 P.M. Everyone knows that, and that is what you would tell a new employee. When the new employee shows up Monday morning at 8:00 and finds that no one else has arrived yet, she begins to discover the group norms. The norm may well be something like "The boss gets here at 8:15 or 8:20. The employees need to get here before the boss." The hypothetical new employee observes this behavior for a few days and generally begins to mimic it. In fact, if she does not, the other employees will let her know in various subtle ways that she is violating a norm. And only a gauche newcomer with no social skills would feel free to comment on the behavior or, worse yet, say to the boss, "I thought you told me we started work at 8:00! No one, including you, comes in at 8:00."

You need to keep in mind that most people will conform to most norms most of the time. They will conform because there is tremendous reinforcement for conforming and considerable pressure on nonconformists. Your job is to do what you can to make sure the group norms are not contrary to the best interests of the organization. There are many, many examples of group norms that establish acceptable productivity levels, for example. New employees are exposed to a variety of verbal and nonverbal harassment if they are perceived as "rate-busters."

Expose the norms. Talk about them in staff meetings. Be aware that you are not even conscious of some of the norms you are following. Ask for help in surfacing them. (You can ask your staff, your boss, a peer, or an outside observer.) Groups establish norms, and they can range from positive through neutral to negative. The more you can work at establishing positive norms, the more effective you will be.

Cooperation and Competition

We spend most of our lives in social exchanges with other people. Through exchanges (of money, time, love, information, services), we establish relationships with the people around us. In these exchanges, we can choose to cooperate (work together toward common goals) or compete (work against each other to gain something at the other's expense).

What determines whether people will choose cooperation or competition? There are five factors that influence that decision:

1. *Our perception of the situation.* We may perceive a win/lose situation and see competition as the only option, when in fact a win/win solution is possible.
2. *The behavior of the other person.* We do not generally behave according to the golden rule (treating others as we would like to be treated). Instead, we treat others the way they treat us, a concept called reciprocity.
3. *Our attributions about people's behavior.* If someone cooperates with us, we will attempt to figure out the cause of his behavior. If we attribute his cooperation to the fact that he is a nice person, we will react differently than if we attribute his cooperation to an attempt to manipulate us.
4. *The number of people involved.* Unfortunately for the movement toward teams in organizations today, we are much more likely to cooperate when we are in one-on-one relationships than when we are in groups. In fact, our tendency toward cooperativeness declines as group size increases.
5. *Our general personality.* Some people are just naturally more competitive than others, and some are more cooperative.

In the midst of all these social exchanges, equity theory would tell us that we are evaluating our relationships on the basis of the relative contributions made and rewards received by each party. We keep track, according to equity theory, of the "fairness" of any relationship. The accountant in your head is comparing the ratio of your gains to your contributions and the ratio of the other person's (or the organization's) gains to contributions.

Since this is a ratio, it is the relative comparisons

that are important. If I gain 10 and contribute 10 and the organization gains 100 and contributes 100, that will seem fair to me. If it is not fair, if my gain is 50 and my contribution is 100 (a ratio of 1:2) and the organization gains 100 and contributes 50 (a ratio of 2), then I will be motivated to change the situation.

The average employee has less control over the gain than over the contribution. He can ask for a raise, but he may not get it. Other ways to increase his gains (e.g., stealing or embezzlement) are dangerous and risky. He has a great deal of control over his contribution, however, and can lessen his efforts by taking longer breaks, not taking work home, calling in sick, or lessening his productivity in a variety of other ways.

As a manager, you need to keep in mind that there is a third way the employee can reach a feeling of equity, and that is by changing his perception of the situation. You can influence the ratio to which he is comparing his own by giving the employee realistic information about the contributions of the organization (perhaps the organization contributes more than he is aware of; for example, he may not realize the value of his health care plan). You can also check out his perceptions about the organization's gains. Perhaps he has some incorrect assumptions about the profit levels the company realizes, for example.

Impressions

When we deal with other people, whether we are meeting them for the first time or work with them on a regular basis, we receive a great deal of information about them. We see things about them, we hear what they say and how they say it, we smell them, we hear what other people have to say about them. What do we do with all these data? We form an impression of the person. In doing so, we set the stage for our later dealings with this person. Sometimes, however, our impressions are wrong.

In our attempts to make sense of all the information we have about someone, we are influenced by some tendencies that are very efficient but not always effective. These tendencies cause us to:

- Give greater weight to information we receive first (the primacy effect). Yes, first impressions are very important, partly because we pay more attention at first; our attention decreases over time.
- Give greater weight to negative than to positive information. This may be a self-protective mechanism, because we have learned to pay more attention to information about someone that may be a threat to us.
- Give greater weight to extreme behaviors, whether positive or negative. An extremely violent or extremely thoughtful action, in other words, will strongly affect our overall impression of someone.
- Give greater weight to information about someone that comes from someone we consider a credible source.
- Give greater weight to unique information than we do to redundant information. If we have seen Jaime act in a thoughtful way several times, seeing another thoughtful act will impress us less than seeing him do something cruel.
- Pay more attention to relevant information. For example, if told that a new employee is lazy and witty, we pay more attention to the "lazy" part. If the person is a new friend of ours, the opposite might apply.

One other influence is our basic disposition. Some of us are inclined to like people in general and view most of them positively; others of us may dislike and be suspicious of people in general.

Overall, how we form impressions of people may tell us more about ourselves than it does about them. As a manager, you are influenced by all the factors we have discussed, even as you formally and informally judge your employees. You are not an unbiased observer of people, even (or especially) when you are filling out their annual evaluations. You can't rid yourself of impressions, but at least be aware of them.

Keep in mind that anytime you receive information about someone, you are actively "processing" that information. Your own frame of reference combines with the available information about the person to form an impression of the person. Check out your assumptions, realize that your impressions may be wrong, and keep yourself open to information that may disconfirm what you "know" about someone. This may sound very simple, but is is very difficult to do. It flies in the face of how we have learned to be.

Prejudice and Discrimination

Prejudice is a negative attitude toward members of some distinct group. Discrimination refers to negative actions toward the member or the group. In this section, we again go back to the roots of concepts, knowing that there are other sources of information for you if you are interested in the legal workplace ramifications of discrimination.

Prejudice is a type of attitude. As we discussed earlier in this chapter, attitudes give us a framework for interpreting information. When we prejudge a person on the basis of the group to which we perceive her to belong, we use the framework to notice and remember only certain things about her, thus reinforcing our prejudice. The tendencies toward prejudice and stereotyping in us are not only cognitive (involving thoughts) but also emotional and behavioral.

Flagrant forms of discrimination have been the focus of legal attention for many years. Most of us have no trouble recognizing flagrant discrimination. The subtle forms, however, often go unnoticed and can do a great deal of damage to workplace relationships and to the office environment.

Subtle discrimination arises from the fact that we see ourselves as belonging to certain groups. You may, for example, see yourself as male, Hispanic, a member of the accounting department, and a manager. We are aware of the groups to which we belong, and we all have subtle biases in favor of our own groups and against others. This tendency is not going to go away. Not all of the cultural diversity workshops and sensitivity training in the world will rid us of this very human tendency. Nor may we wish to get rid of it altogether. It is a force for cohesion and team spirit that can be very beneficial in organizations. What do we need to do, then? We need to be aware that we are all biased. Once we have identified a group (the personnel department, women, Asians, short people, joggers), we tend to assume that all its members are more alike than they really are and that they are somehow "different" from members of other groups. We must constantly consciously remind ourselves of the arbitrariness of these groupings.

We must also be aware of the forms of subtle discrimination that are going on around us all the time. Some forms of discrimination include:

- *A reluctance to help.* We are very good at refusing assistance to "outsiders" and making it appear very reasonable ("Purchasing isn't really my area. I shouldn't interfere in your department").

- *Tokenism.* We "prove" our broad-mindedness by taking some small, even trivial, positive action toward a member of another group. We then use this action to justify refusing any real help ("I gave my secretary a plant on Secretary's Day. I don't think I need to send her to this seminar on how to get ahead in organizations"). You can see why subtle discrimination is not something we do consciously! Its rationale often doesn't survive logical thought.
- *Cross-group stereotyping.* A member of a particular group is seen as looking, acting, or thinking like all other members of the group ("We can't offer him the promotion. The position involves travel, and he is a single parent").

Subtle discrimination is taking place right now in your workplace. You do it, and so does everyone else. It should be evident by now that we are not talking about just the usual discriminatory actions (based on gender, age, or ethnicity) but a problem involving all of the subtle groupings we make (white-collar versus blue-collar; cross-department, cross-functional, and cross-level stereotypes). In addition to simple awareness, one accepted way to combat discrimination is to increase contact between two groups. The era of cross-functional teams, for example, should usher in more understanding and appreciation between functions. It is important that the contact take place in a context of equal status and cooperation, however, or prejudices may be reinforced.

The Best Team Possible: Part 2

In the scenario that opened this chapter, you brought Jill, Bob, Mark, and Adam together to complete an important project. Although they are all top performers, they had not worked together before, and your lack of attention to the interpersonal issues caused you to be surprised by their lack of progress.

Bob and Mark are acting aggressively toward each other. Bob has formed an impression of Adam that is affecting their work together. Mark is making a bid for power, and Adam is drawing gender-based conclusions about Jill.

Although you may be tempted to tell them all to grow up and get to work, it is essential that you help them lay the groundwork for effective teamwork. As we will see in Chapter 8, effective teamwork is not just something that comes naturally to people. It requires an investment of time and energy on your part to make sure that it occurs.

What Do You Need to Know About Social Psychology?

One of the recurring themes of this chapter has been self-awareness. Many of the factors that influence the interaction between people are not conscious, and awareness is a constant struggle. Surface your own awareness, work on that of those around you, and be aware of the constant pull of norms, attitudes, impressions, and prejudice.

Aggression is aroused in you by certain factors. You have deeply ingrained attitudes that affect how you behave toward other people. You make attributions about other people's behavior and form impressions of them that may or may not be accurate. Your tendencies toward conformity are influenced by the norms of your work groups. You strive for a balance between cooperation and competition. You also hold prejudices and discriminate in ways that are subtle or flagrant.

Sometimes managers think that they are "different" because they are managers. You are more like your employees than you are unlike them, regardless of your title. You are influenced by all the factors that influence them, and are just as human. Take a look at yourself, apply the knowledge in this chapter to yourself, and then use it to manage people more effectively.

Manager's Checklist

☐ When dealing with aggression, keep in mind:
  • Factors that arouse aggression
    —Frustration
    —Provocation
    —Exposure
    —Arousal
    —Environmental factors
  • Handling aggression
    —Don't reinforce it
    —Punish it
    —Arrange for training in social skills
    —Arouse an incompatible response

☐ Two ways to change people's attitudes:
  • Persuasion
  • Dissonance

☐ When making attributions about other people's behavior, be aware of:
  • Internal causes
  • External causes
  • Fundamental attribution error

☐ To constructively use the concepts of conformity in your work group:
  • Identify norms

☐ Whether cooperation or competition occurs is influenced by:
  • Our perception of the situation
  • The behavior of the other person
  • Our attributions about people's behavior
  • The number of people involved
  • Our general personality

☐ When forming impressions, we give greater weight to:
  • Information we got first
  • Negative information
  • Extreme behaviors
  • Information from what we consider a credible source
  • Unique information
  • Relevant information

☐ Subtle forms of prejudice/discrimination include:
  • A reluctance to help
  • Tokenism
  • Cross-group stereotyping

8

"Works and Plays Well With Others" —*Group Behavior, Teams, and Leadership*

Two heads are better than one, right? Of course, a camel is a horse designed by a committee. When we have two such conflicting pieces of conventional wisdom to guide us, how do we decide whether to have an individual or a group perform a task or make a decision? We know that groups do influence their members' behavior, but how?

Many organizations have embraced the team concept as the way to organize in the 1990s. The difficult part of the movement toward teams, self-directed and otherwise, is that people behave differently when around other people. Four top producers may not turn into your top-producing team when you make them work together. On the other hand, marginal workers may shine when given a different set of teammates. In this chapter, we explore group dynamics, teams, and leadership.

The Project Team: Part 1

Janice, Paul, Marcie, and Emily have been pulled off their regular assignments to work on a special task force that will be preparing the marketing campaign for a new release of a popular software package. In their "regular" jobs, they all report to different people. Rather than fit their project into the existing organizational structure, the executive team decided to let the four employees form a self-managed project team, with no formal leader.

At first, everything seemed to go fairly well. The four met over coffee to formulate their first plans, set timetables, and sort out tasks. The meeting was congenial, friendly, and upbeat. By the second meeting, however, things began to go wrong. There were accusations from Janice and Paul of "bossiness" on Marcie's part. Emily's opinion was that someone had to take charge, and it might as well be Marcie. Paul had not completed the tasks he had agreed to have done and said it was because he disagreed with the timetable they had set at the first meeting.

Within a few days, Janice had begun taking work home, completing it there and then presenting her results to the other three as a finished product. Emily became very quiet and withdrawn and quit volunteering any information except to agree with anything Marcie said. Paul and Marcie were engaged in subtle personal attacks, including efforts to get the other two to take sides. Before one of their meetings, Marcie called Janice and Emily to tell them that the meeting location had been changed, but "forgot" to tell Paul.

Before we figure out what to do about this team, let's consider what we know about group dynamics, teams, group development, and leadership.

Group Dynamics

We know quite a bit about the differences in behavior between individuals and groups. First, there is the concept of *social facilitation*. People's behavior changes simply because of the presence of others. If you are performing a task, you will do it either better or worse when people are around than you would if you were by yourself. Not much help so far, is it? Research into this phenomenon has shown that the presence of other people (and the possibility that they might be evaluating you) causes a general increase in tension or arousal. If you are performing a task that is simple and easy for you, the arousal will cause you to do it better. If the tasks is complicated or hard, you will perform less well.

There are a few other terms that are key to understanding group behavior. The concept of *deindividuation* describes the ability of groups to weaken the restraints of its members against engaging in impulsive behavior. This has also been called the mob effect and may have to do with the lessening of individual responsibility felt when one is in a crowd. Keep in mind that a team effort results in a diminished sense of responsibility in each individual member of the team.

Risky shift refers to an individual's increased tendency to take risks or make risky decisions after discussion with a group. In the workplace, this goes hand-in-hand with the deindividuation effect. When you throw a decision out to a group to make, members will take more risks as a group than they would as individuals. Notice that this does not mean the decision will be of higher or lower quality; you will still need to decide what risks are appropriate in a given situation.

Social loafing means that individual efforts decrease as the group size increases. Explanations of social loafing are based on the fact the any one person will see her individual efforts as less essential as the group gets larger. Since there is a lot of research to back up the concept of social loafing, give some thought to the implications when you embrace teamwork. There are pros and cons to teamwork; this is one of the downsides.

There are several things that a manager needs to understand about *group cohesiveness*. Cohesiveness arises out of group members' attraction to one another and their motivation to belong to the group. Cohesiveness can be a very positive force, and it can also be quite dysfunctional. A group that is too cohesive may come to value itself as a group more than it values making good decisions. Such a group may well show no conflict or disagreement and therefore make poor decisions. Its cohesiveness may also attach to common goals, such as "do as little work as possible without being caught," that clearly are in conflict with the organization's goals.

A group that makes poor decisions because its main goal is to avoid conflict among its members is enmeshed in *groupthink*. First identified by the psychologist Irving Janus, groupthink refers to the tendency of groups to rationalize poor decisions, exert a pressure on members to conform with the group, and create the illusion of unanimity (because no one will speak up to disagree). Have you ever left a meeting where everyone agreed on a course of action, thinking to yourself, "Well, I don't think it's going to work, but everyone else seemed so sure I hated to throw cold water on the idea"? If so, you have engaged in groupthink. When a colleague approaches you over coffee and says, "Boy, that idea stinks, doesn't it?" and you agree, did you ever question why neither of you spoke up in the meeting? Groupthink is the answer.

As a manager, should you appoint a group or an individual to solve a problem or make a decision? There are several factors to consider. Group decisions take more time. Do you have the time to give to the group? If the building is on fire (literally or figuratively), you may have to make an autocratic decision and bark out orders. Group decisions generate more commitment from the group to the plan of action chosen. Is it critical that you have group support for a new way of doing things? Then you can't afford not to include others in the planning process. Once you give a task to a group, make sure you've given it the resources it needs to get the job done and access to the people it needs help from. In addition to information, the group members may need training on group processes or on how to make effective decisions. Delegating to a group is much like delegating to individuals; it does not mean that you let the group flounder. Make sure members are prepared and able to do the task, let them decide on the means to get there, and help them over the rough spots they encounter.

Groups and Teams

Think about a time you were a member of a high-performing team, whether it was a work group, a sports team, or any other kind of team. Those times of high performance carry with them a feeling of exhilaration that is hard to match.

Every group, of course, is not a team. The basic definitions of teams include such qualities as a common purpose, a sense of commitment to the group's goals, and a sense of responsibility to one another. Teams are relatively stable and at least somewhat interdependent. If a group of people is able to set goals, analyze and solve problems, implement the solutions, and feel responsible for its output, it is a true team.

High-performing teams are characterized by high levels of open communication, trust, optimism about what they can do, high expectations of themselves, participation by all members, and a dedication to common goals. Unfortunately, high-performing teams are somewhat rare. Obviously, you can't send people to a seminar on how to trust each other; trust has to develop over time (and sometimes fails to develop). You can, however, teach people about these characteristics and give them some help in specific skills, such as communication.

High-performing teams sometimes develop without any help from the manager. It's tempting to attribute this to luck and keep your fingers crossed that it continues. It is far more helpful, of course, to figure out why and how it developed and to replicate those conditions as much as possible in other teams.

Stages of Team Development

Effective teams develop by coming to grips with both the task at hand and the social interactions of the group. Both the social process and the task focus are important, and what is needed is an appropriate balance between the two.

Orientation

The first stage of group development involves *orientation*. The social interaction is quiet and polite, and the task focus revolves around orienting to the problem. The orientation phase involves getting information about the task and about the other people involved. People are asking themselves, "What is it we have to do?" and "Where do I fit in?"

The orientation phase may be short, or it may last a while, depending on the nature of the group and the task at hand. To the impatient manager, the lesson is this: The team members will need to spend some time orienting themselves to the task and to one another. This is not time wasted but time invested in turning out a higher quality product.

Conflict

As the group begins to organize itself, interpersonal and task *conflicts* almost always arise. It is essential that the group work through the conflicts, learning how to disagree without personality clashes and how to utilize the viewpoints of each member.

Sometimes in this stage there is a sense of dissatisfaction, a feeling that "I could do this easier by myself." The conflict stage is the most difficult, both for the team members and for the manager. Some groups stall at this point; others, given the right amounts of encouragement, support, and specific conflict resolution skills, move on. As the manager, you need to help the team distinguish between healthy conflict and unhealthy, unproductive conflict. The team also needs to learn how to handle conflict constructively.

Lessons learned in this stage include the fact that it is healthy to disagree, that it is not healthy to attack each other personally, and that the best solution is often a combination of ideas from all members of the group. Again, as in the first stage, it is important to spend enough time here so that these important lessons can be learned.

Norms

The third stage involves gathering the information and resources needed to complete the task or make the decision, and the formation of group standards and *norms*, or "how we work together." At this point, the group is able to generate ideas as well as data to expedite its work. As the manager, watch the development of norms. If the group seems to avoid conflict (feeling a little bruised after the conflict stage), it may need some help in letting all of the creative conflict come out. One norm will determine the level of productivity the group achieves or considers appropriate. Again, keep an eye on the appropriateness of that level.

Group norms have a very powerful effect on group productivity. This effect can be either positive for the organization, supporting increased productivity, or negative for the organization if it decreases productivity. The group's goals may be opposed to those of the organization, and the group's goals may take precedence. Suppose you have a group working for you that has always prided itself on its high level of performance. If a new person transfers into this group, the group will communicate to him in subtle and not-so-subtle ways that a certain level of performance is expected of him. In a crew that stocked the shelves at night in a large supermarket, a new member was considered to be not a very hard worker. The group teased, prodded, and otherwise urged him to work faster ("Boy, is my back tired!" "Why?" "From carrying Bill all night!" "Tomorrow I'll have to remember my saddle"). When these tactics didn't work, the group ostracized Bill. They didn't talk to him or eat lunch with him, and they frequently asked the supervisor to give him tasks that would require him to work alone. Bill eventually transferred to another store in the chain.

The opposite effect can also occur. In a team of computer programmers, a newcomer was told to slow down. It took the guise of teasing ("There's Jill again, working through the break. Are you dedicated or what?"). When she didn't get the message, it got more pointed ("We're going for coffee now. Come with us"). She got the message, and when she slowed down some, the group rewarded her by being much more sociable toward her. Some groups go so far as to tell the newcomer to slow down, that she is making them all look bad, but most of the time this norm is reinforced more subtly. The threat of ostracism from the group is frequently more important to people than the manager's standards, and, as in this example, the group's goals come to take precedence over the organization's.

Interdependence

The fourth and final stage in a team's development involves problem solving, true *interdependence,* and high levels of participation and cooperation. A team at this stage deals constructively with conflict, using it for its creative possibilities and not letting it become destructive. As manager, you take on more of a support role, since the team is providing its own direction and encouragement.

Notice that at each stage, both the task and the interpersonal work have to be done. You need to allow the time for the social system to develop, as well as the technical and task work. If your organization is to benefit from the team approach, recognize that the people side of teamwork is far more than just "the soft stuff" and in fact is a vital part of the mix that makes teams so valuable.

As a manager, you need to realize that group work is more effective when time is allowed for appropriate team development. Team problems, such as a sense of uncertainty in the orientation phase or frustration in the second stage where conflict is common, are often simply part of the phase and not permanent. The trick is to know when to intervene and when to let the team alone. If conflict is emotional or damaging or if it becomes a pattern, you may want to provide the team with some conflict management skills. Be careful about jumping in prematurely, however; working through the conflict is an important part of the team's learning.

The manager's job is gradually to work herself out

of a job when it comes to managing groups. In the orientation phase, you will be taking a more directive approach and providing fairly close supervision. As the team progresses, you may move into a less active role, help the group think through decisions rather than make them, and gradually begin to give the group wider responsibility. If the group members progress to the final stages of true team performance, you can delegate comfortably to them. In fact, close supervision will be more a hindrance and annoyance at this point than it will be a help.

The developmental process is probably easiest to manage with intact work groups that will be together until someone quits. With ad hoc task forces, committees, or other shorter-term teams, the termination phase must also be considered. When a team has experienced great success or has stalled, it sometimes needs help pulling the plug. Have you ever been on a team that continued to meet after its job was done or when the objective was so fuzzy that no one knew if the work was done or not? The camaraderie that develops in a high-performing team is often hard to let go of. If disbanded, the team may plan reunions, lunches, and other get-togethers to keep in touch. Sometimes, the team simply doesn't disband but keeps meeting every Tuesday morning over donuts and coffee. The lesson for the manager is that every short-term team should have clear starting and ending points, either a time frame or an end goal. It may need your help again toward the end to meet those goals and disband, because members may feel a certain reluctance to do so, particularly if they have been successful.

Leadership

There is so much written on leadership, so many books, newsletters, and seminars, that you have undoubtedly been exposed to a great deal on this topic. If you have not, this section may be a good place to start, but it is not an all-inclusive review of leadership theory. This section stays true to our initial purpose, which is to look at the basics of research in psychology and social psychology and to turn those basics into practical lessons for managing other people.

The focus of this chapter is team psychology. We look at leadership in terms of the relationship between leaders and followers. If you are a manager, you have a certain position given to you by the organizational hierarchy, you have some power, and you have some subordinates. You may or may not be a leader.

The focus of leadership research is twofold: who becomes a leader and what factors determine leadership success. The first has somewhat less practical value for our purposes, but, in a nutshell, here is what the research says.

Some personal traits are correlated with emerging as a leader. These traits include height, physical attractiveness, intelligence, self-confidence, and talkativeness. Of course, there are tall, attractive, talkative people who do not become leaders. That is because there are also situational factors that determine leadership. Research in this area shows that the situational factors interact with the personal traits to determine who emerges as a leader.

If you are already a manager, it may be of more interest to you to look at what factors determine leader success. How should you act if you want to be a good leader and have the people working for you be satisfied and productive? The answer is that it depends on the situation. There are two dimensions to leader behavior that have emerged over and over again in research: the degree of focus on the task at hand and the degree of focus on the people and the relationships. The most successful leaders can read the situation and decide when they need the people focus and when they should stay focused on the task. In very difficult situations or crises, an effective leader takes charge and gets the job done. (If the building is on fire, he does not ask how everyone feels about evacuating.) In very slow times or with easy tasks, an effective leader may also be quite task-focused, lest the team fall into lethargy. The relationship focus is the most effective leader behavior when times are neither too tough nor too easy. The key for leaders is to be adaptable and flexible and to have the ability to "read" situations.

Keep in mind that leadership and followership are reciprocal relationships. You cannot be a leader without followers; you need them as much as or more than they need you. How you influence your followers relates to their job satisfaction and their productivity. Your areas of influence include:

• *Modeling.* Your behavior, good or bad, serves as a model for the people who work for you. People tend to pattern their behavior after their leader's behavior, and what you do is far more important than what you say.

• *Managing expectations.* Good leaders tend to have high expectations of people, and people tend to live up to them. There is another example of the self-fulfilling prophecy, which we discussed in Chapter 3. It is not necessary that you communicate verbally your positive or negative expectations to people for the self-fulfilling prophecy to work, so be careful if you are the type of manager who thinks that people in general are lazy or unproductive.

• *Communicating.* Leaders are good communicators. They are aware of the impact of the words they use, they provide opportunities for two-way communication, they have good listening skills, they are seen as a good source of information by their followers, and they are seen as trustworthy. In a sense, their communication skills tend to clarify the role of the follower so that the follower can move forward confidently in fulfilling that role. (Chapter 9 covers communication in much more detail.)

Keep in mind that leaders help to determine the job satisfaction and the productivity of their followers. If you have subordinates who are "lazy, unproductive, and unhappy," take a look at your own leadership style first.

Leading Teams

There are at least three factors to consider when you lead a team: whether or not it is even appropriate for a work task to be done by a team; how to create an environment that allows the team to do its best work; and how to provide the best leadership for the team.

As a manager, you are faced with delegating tasks on a regular basis. In today's organizations, it is often assumed that teamwork is the correct way to approach a task. The real answer, of course, is not that simple. If teamwork leads to an open exchange of information and insight, creativity, and innovation, the group's decision is likely to be a good one. If teamwork leads to conflict, ego battles, and disagreement over goals, the group's decision is likely to be a bad one.

In general, if conflict can be properly managed, group decisions tend to be of higher quality than decisions made by any one individual. In addition, people's acceptance of and commitment to the decision is higher. The biggest cost is the investment of time required. It is always faster to delegate a decision to one person or to make it yourself than it is to convene a meeting and try to reach consensus on a decision. It is up to you to decide which decisions warrant this investment in time. If the decision requires commitment and support from the people involved, then it pays to have the people involved in the decision.

Creating the right kind of environment for a team requires understanding the elements of a supportive team atmosphere. When you think back to your experiences with high-performing teams or ask current teams about their successes, you will find that they have some elements in common. First, teams need to have the necessary resources made available to them. Of course, no organization has unlimited resources. But, while teams can be creative and innovative on small budgets, there needs to be a threshold amount of time, tools, money, and other resources available to them.

Second, teams that feel part of the big picture in an organization are often motivated to achieve high goals. A manager's role is to make sure that the goals, objectives, vision, and mission of an organization are communicated to and understood by all employees.

Third, the organizational structure itself should not get in the way of good teamwork. While that sounds obvious, many organizations establish teams and then do nothing about old reward systems, compensation decisions, chains of command, and other issues that can get in the way of teamwork. If an organization asks for teamwork but rewards people on the basis of their individual achievements, the results will be destructive competition.

What specific actions can managers take to create the right kind of environment? First, know your team members. Know their skills and abilities and their developmental stage, so that you can decide on the appropriate level of involvement for you to take. Solving problems for them will annoy them if they are an established team; delegating too early is just as damaging. Recognize their achievements, and do what you can to publicize their achievements to your boss and to the larger organization. Keep them posted as to what is going on in the company; remember, they need to know the "big picture."

The Project Team: Part 2

The team example that opened this chapter describes a fairly common set of occurrences. In the name of "self-management," a team with an important job to do was allowed to flounder.

The experiences of the team so far are predictable and typical. The orientation phase went well, with politeness and congeniality all around. The conflict stage, however, is threatening to undermine the team and lead to its ultimate failure.

People are not prepared to work on teams unless you, the manager, prepare them. It's similar to a situation you may have experienced when you were promoted to your first supervisory position. It was assumed that you knew how to supervise, that you had somehow picked up the ability through osmosis. If you ask people to work on a team, tell them what you mean by that. Discover what skills they will need that they do not have now. Provide guidance in those skills.

Janice, Paul, Marcie, and Emily needed help at the point at which we left off. The vice president of marketing, who was the executive most closely tied to the project, decided to take a hand when he heard rumors of the problems. He first took the team back to square one in terms of the organization's expectations of them, the skills each one had that caused him or her to be chosen for the assignment, and the way in which it was expected that the members would work together. He then provided the team with some training on how to structure its meetings, how to write action plans, and how to pursue consensus when conflicts arose.

With the executive's help, the team was able to pull out of the conflict stage having learned some new skills and renegotiated some of its roles. It was able to enter the third and the fourth stages, not conflict-free but with some specific techniques to manage and take advantage of the creativity of conflict.

What Do You Need to Know About Teams?

There are times when it is appropriate to form a team and times when it is not appropriate. The mix of people, skills, knowledge, and personalities on the team is important, although people prefer to work with others who are like them. There are predictable stages that a team will go through, and you need to watch for danger signals that show you the team needs help. True to our view of management as a balancing act, there are times when you should not intervene.

Manager's Checklist

☐ When you are deciding whether to have an individual or a group perform a task or make a decision, ask yourself the following questions:
  • How committed to the decision do I need people to be?
  • How much time do we have?
  • How important are creativity and innovation to the project?

☐ When the team is being formed, ask:
  • Who do I need on the team, in terms of skills (technical and interpersonal), knowledge, and creativity?
  • Is there a good balance of personalities?

☐ As the team is doing its work, ask:
  • Is there unproductive conflict going on?
  • What else does the team need from me to be productive?

9

"I Know You Think You Understand What You Thought I Said" —*Communication*

In the section on attitudes in Chapter 7, we talked about persuasion, one type of communication. In this chapter, we take a broader look at communication and the underlying human frailties that make effective and efficient communication tough in organizations.

The Forbidden Snack Bar: Part 1

In a large grocery store, employees who were going on a break had two choices for purchasing a cold soda. They could buy a can from the refrigerated drink section, or they could buy soda in a cup, with ice, from the snack bar inside the store. The new store manager preferred that employees buy the soda in cans, because that way the store got credit for the sale instead of the outside company that ran the snack bar.

During one of his first visits to the store, the new manager passed an employee drinking a soda from a cup. "Don't buy from the snack bar," he said. Within hours, the

word had gotten out: The new manager, for reasons unknown, did not want employees to purchase anything from
the snack bar. For weeks, employees were going to nearby
fast food chains for breaks and lunch periods, accepting
the new "rule" without asking why. Only when the assistant
manager heard about the "rule" and asked the manager
about it was the misunderstanding brought to light.

What Is Communication?

In a broad and therefore less than helpful definition, everything you do, say, wear, don't do, and so on communicates something in an organization. Communication is
a form of behavior, and every behavior is a communication.

Communication is also an organizational process
that can be looked at as a series of steps taken to dissemi-
nate information. It involves creating, displaying, and
interpreting messages. Someone (the sender) does something (the message) in a way (the medium) that gets
someone else's attention (the receiver), and there is a result (feedback).

Characteristics of the Sender

Suppose you wish to send a message to your staff. As
we discussed in Chapter 7, your credibility is an issue
here. In a broader sense, of course, everything about you
is at issue here. If you send a memo, have a meeting,
send an E-mail, or otherwise deliver a message, your
past relationship with the people involved will play a big
part in determining how they receive the message. If the
message is delivered to people who don't know you,
they will immediately form an impression (accurate or
otherwise) of you through whatever information is avail-

able to them. If you are making a speech, for example, your clothing, grooming, accent, and physical appearance will influence the message. Before you think, "That isn't right! I would judge a message on its own merits!," keep in mind that you are incapable of freeing yourself from just this kind of impression formation. What you can do is be aware that your reaction to a message is being influenced by all these extraneous things.

Characteristics of the Message

What about the communication itself? The choice of words is very important. It is not mere semantics to note the difference between saying.

**All employees will work mandatory overtime
until further notice.**

and

Due to a large, seasonal increase in orders, it will be necessary for all employees to work overtime for the next two weeks. Thank you for your cooperation.

In the second example, a reason is given (the increase in orders) and a time frame is communicated (two weeks). The first message will raise these kinds of questions in employees' minds and will be likely to arouse resistance. The second message, while not ensuring 100 percent compliance, will at least provide the initial information that employees will want to know.

The frequency and the repetitiveness of a message also influence the way in which it is received. If something is important to you, you need to communicate it frequently and in as many ways as possible. If your message to your employees is that customers are important, a memo to that point will likely fall flat. If you send a memo, arrange for classes in customer service, spend time with customers yourself, and show by many and varied actions that you believe that customers are important, the message will be received.

Characteristics of the Medium

When you choose to write a memo, deliver a message in person, or frown at a person who is engaging in behavior you don't care for, you are choosing a medium for your message. Which way(s) is best? The answer, of course, is, "That depends." Various message formats are more or less effective under different circumstances. Ask yourself what it is you are trying to communicate and what seems the appropriate medium.

The first question to ask yourself may revolve around what is available to you. What choices do you have? It makes a difference if a message is sent via memo, a speech, voice mail, or a personal phone call. In many organizations today, the simple fact that E-mail is available may cause it to be a favored medium. The fact is that there are appropriate and inappropriate mediums for any kind of message.

How urgent is the message? Considerations here are the speed of communication, the overload on the channel, and the sense of urgency that can be conveyed in one media versus another. An urgent message obviously needs to be sent in the fastest possible way, right? Maybe. If the fastest way is extremely expensive, you may opt for the second- or third-fastest, as long as the message will still be delivered. Are there channels of communication in your organization that are overloaded, such as voice mail? If so, an urgent message may get lost there, and you may wish to choose an alternate method. The "sense of urgency" question is best answered by your own knowledge of your organization. As with overload, a message sent via a medium that is overused is more likely to be ignored. But if the medium is a personal visit from the CEO to your office, you will sense immediately that the message is important (especially if she has never, in the ten years you've worked there, been seen in your office).

What impact are you looking to have on the recipients of your message? A razzle-dazzle video teleconference will have more impact than a memo. If your message is important, it needs to look important.

What are the costs of the various options? The razzle-dazzle teleconference may meet your needs at times, but you'll go broke using it for all messages (not to mention the fact that it will lose its impact if it is a daily occurrence).

Do you need a response? Some messages are easier to respond to than others. If responses are required, make that clear, and make it simple to respond.

Characteristics of the Receiver

A receiver interprets your message. The key point here is that this interpretation is the only message that counts. It is also the one over which you have the least amount of direct control! If you craft your image, your message, and your medium very carefully, your message may still be misinterpreted. That's why the feedback loop is so important. Two-way communication allows for feedback and confirmation of the message. If you are delivering a message to a group (your staff, perhaps), anticipate some of the objections or reactions on the basis of your knowledge of your listeners, and plan for their reactions.

More generally, you need to know the audience. For a speech, a memo, or other communication that is going out to a large number of people, it is vital to research and take into account the background, skill level, and ability to receive of the audience. One large hotel in southern California sent out an urgent memo to all employees, somehow overlooking the fact that a large percentage of the employees spoke only broken English and were not able to read written English. An engineering department sent out important information about a new product, but the other employees who had no engineering background could not comprehend the information. A telecommunications firm conveyed time-sensitive information by way of voice mail, even though close to half of its employees worked out in the field and had no office or phone.

Everything we've talked about in this book (perception, personality, learning, motives, attitudes) also affects the receiver of a communication. Remember when we said that we tend to perceive what we expect to perceive? I was working with a management group on improving communication, and one of the first things I did was observe a staff meeting. The participants were trying to solve a problem. One person, Jim, had the right answer. He said it once, and no one paid any attention. He said it a second time. No one acknowledged him. At that point, he gave up and did not speak again. I found out later that the perception of the group was that Jim never contributed in meetings. Because of this perception, the group literally did not hear him when he did try to communicate.

A similar thing happens when a group perceives that a member never contributes anything of value. In this case, the individual may express an opinion or idea, only to have it ignored or attacked. Minutes, days, or months later, someone else expresses the same opinion or idea, and the group enthusiastically adopts it. This may have happened to you, as it is fairly common. The person who expresses the message in this case is more important than the message itself. Another example of this is an idea expressed by the boss and admired by everyone, when it's obvious that if a person of lesser power had expressed the same idea, it would have had no support.

Characteristics of the Feedback

A feedback loop built into your communication processes allows you to check that the message has been received and that it has had its intended result. Feedback allows for two-way communication, which is almost always more accurate and more effective than one-way.

How you get feedback depends to a great extent upon the medium used. If you are talking to one person face-to-face, you are getting feedback throughout the message delivery by way of the person's nonverbal behavior. Does your listener look puzzled, excited, or bored? (Be sure to check out your assumption about what her facial expression means.) You can also, of course, invite comment or ask the person to restate what she understood you to say. You have less data to work with in a phone conversation and even less in an E-mail conversation, even if it is two-way.

Communicating to groups has its own challenges. If you send a memo to the 4,000 people in your company or address them at a meeting, how do you arrange for feedback? Here, the message and the medium interact to give you guidance as to the best method to employ. How important is the message? How vital is it that everyone understand the details of the message? How much time and money do you have to invest? How much would it cost if a percentage of the employees did not understand? You may decide, after considering all of these factors, that a series of small group meetings would be more effective and allow for questions and comments to be made. On the other hand, you may decide that a memo to all employees, including the line "If you have any questions or comments, please call Martha at extension 1234," would suffice. The bottom line is that you should choose the most appropriate method(s), given the importance of effectiveness and efficiency in a given situation.

Characteristics of the Direction

In addition to the process of communication, it is important to consider the various directions this process can take. The three major directions that communication can take in an organization are up, down, and horizontal.

How do you and the other managers in your organization get information from lower-level employees? How do you communicate with your boss and your boss's boss? Many organizations have some type of employee opinion survey to collect formal data that will be communicated upward. Others tout open-door policies that promise open communication among all levels. Many things interfere with effective upward communication in organizations, not the least of which is lack of trust. Think about a manufacturing manager whose staff has informed her that a new piece of recently purchased machinery does not perform the way the staff had hoped. There are many reasons why the manager might distort this message when it is time to pass it on to her boss. If the manager was involved in the decision to buy the machinery, she might be concerned that it will reflect badly on her judgment or on the depth of research she did before making the purchase. A message that starts out to be pretty straightforward ("The new machine doesn't do what we need it to do") becomes a little distorted as it travels upward ("There are a few minor bugs we have to work out with the new machine") and quite distorted by the time it reaches the executive suite ("Looks like the new machine is working fine"). Note that what started out as a deliberate "softening" of the message has been passed along as an honest representation of what the individual thinks he has heard.

Downward communication has its own set of problems. These problems range from management's beliefs about people ("They wouldn't understand this complicated information") to information overload. If you have a full in-box daily, voice mail messages waiting each time you take a coffee break, and E-mail that takes an hour to read through after lunch, you have information overload. How exactly are you supposed to pick out the important data from the rest?

The whole idea of horizontal communication in organizations has recently become of great interest, as organizations begin to think in terms of cross-functional processes and process teams. You may need to share information with your peers in an organization, coordinate work, or negotiate differences. Distortions in horizontal communication may take place when there is competition between departments, "turfism," or simply geographical separation that makes clear communication difficult.

Characteristics of the Organization

Every organization has a culture or a climate within which communication takes place. Think about the climate of your organization. Is it warm or cold? Is it open or guarded? These factors have a great deal of influence on the amount, direction, and openness of the communication.

If you wrote down all the words that described your organization, what would that list look like? Imagine the difference between an organization described as "formal, conservative, cold, slow, paranoid" and an organization described as "fun, loose, family atmosphere, caring." Would you expect the communication patterns to be quite different from one organization to the next?

One of the requirements if open communication is to take place in an organization is a high level of trust. Trust involves issues like the organization's reaction to failure, risk taking, and honesty. Communication can quickly become squelched in the absence of trust. A manager's job involves making sure that the atmosphere of the organization is conducive to open communication. Otherwise, all of the techniques and seminars in the world won't help open up the channels of communication.

Barriers to Effective Communication

Most of the barriers to effective communication in organizations are the result of one of two problems: distortions of various kinds in the communications process and the information overload that faces us every day.

Distortions occur because of all of the individual differences that we have been talking about throughout this book. We are all different in our life experiences, our frames of reference, the selective perceptions we engage in, the value judgments we make, and the filters we use to communicate. When you think about it, it's amazing that any communication takes place at all. Even addressing a small staff of eight people, a manager is talking to people with eight different frames of reference, each of whom puts his or her own interpretation on the message.

Anyone who works in organizations today is familiar with the concept of overload. Whatever your level in an organization, you are faced with a tremendous amount of information each day. A typical manager's desk has an in-box (usually overflowing with memos and reports), a stack of trade or professional journals, a phone with the message light blinking, and a PC with the E-mail indicator on and Internet access. The calendar of this typical manager's day is filled with meetings, business lunches, and presentations. Unfortunately (or fortunately), human nature responds to overload by shutting down. How can you communicate in a way that makes your memo stand out from all the other, less important, memos in your staff's in-boxes? How do you communicate urgency in a voice mail that is thirteenth in a queue of twenty-five waiting after lunch?

Improving Communication

There are several areas to address when you want to improve the communications in your organization: analysis, follow-up, repetition, style, timing, regulating, and listening.

Analysis

Before undertaking efforts to improve communications, it is essential to do a thorough analysis of the current situation. What is the current state of affairs in your organization? What would you prefer it to be? What is the gap between the current state and what you would like? Analyzing this gap allows you to spend time and money on the real problem, instead of on quick fixes or Band-Aid solutions. Analysis allows you to devise a solution that works; solutions like training, development, performance management, or a change in the organizational structure itself work best when they are fitted to the problem.

The director of a major division in a manufacturing firm, for example, felt that the managers who reported to him were allowing too many things to fall between the cracks. While each department did its job, the hand-offs between departments did not take place in an organized fashion. The director arranged for a team-building session for the managers in the division in an attempt to increase cohesiveness and mutual understanding. While the team-building session was enjoyable, nothing changed once the participants all went back to work. The problem was not team cohesiveness. The director then arranged for training in project management and cross-functional process improvement. While the training was interesting and informative, it did not improve the situation. With a large sum already invested in training and development, the director decided that maybe he was facing a performance issue and not a training issue at all. He fired one of the managers and replaced her with someone he felt could do the job better. You guessed it; no results. Finally, the director realized that the communication problem was a result of how his division was structured. The communication channels were all funneled through him, the managers had no daily contact, and their reward systems were set up in a way that ensured competition instead of cooperation. The solution to the communication problem was a structural one.

This example is not unusual in that it took a lot of time and money to hit on the real solution. The power of doing the analysis beforehand is that you will spend time and money on a solution that works.

Follow-Up

Follow-up is an essential part of all important communications, whether one-on-one or group. If it is essential that your message be received and understood, you must establish a feedback channel to determine the reception and comprehension.

Your follow-up efforts depend on the importance of the communication. You can't do extensive follow-up on every memo. Ask yourself what you need to know. Do you need confirmation that the individual received your message? Do you need a reply? Do you need confirmation that the message was understood correctly?

Repetition

Repetition is a method for improving the reception of communications. You can follow a memo by a voice mail, or you can repeat a meeting agenda item in a memo. Not only is repetition powerful, but the use of a variety of media makes it likely that you'll reach more people.

As with follow-up, the use of repetition is based on the importance of the message. Constant repetition of daily, mundane messages is boring, pointless, and costly. Repetition of an important message is powerful. If you are trying to change deep-seated beliefs or values in an organization, repetition is your best opportunity. Years ago, a monopolistic public utility began to instill a value of customer service. It was an uphill struggle, since employees had never been asked to think in that fashion before. It took several years to change the climate of the organization, with constant repetition of the message that employees were now expected to place a high value on customer service. The message was everywhere—posters, newsletters, memos, and recognition programs. In addition, executives went out into the field with technicians to talk with customers. Every company event was used as a forum to repeat the message. Contests were held for employees to come up with customer-based slogans, and recognition was given for individual acts of high-quality customer service.

Style

Pay attention to the style of your communication and to the level of employee that will be receiving the communication. A formal style, for example, will be effective with some audiences and ineffective with others. If you prefer a very casual style, ask yourself how appropriate that is in a given context. As we have said before, flexibility and adaptability are important attributes of an effective manager. Be willing to change your style when necessary for effective communication.

A delicate balance is required; while you by no means wish to appear to be talking down to people, you also need to avoid talking over their heads. The best advice is to know your audience and to communicate plainly and clearly. If you are preparing a memo or a speech, get a few people to look over your final product to be sure that you are communicating what you intended to communicate. And don't just ask people who think and talk like you to look at it. Ask someone from outside your area of specialization or someone from your target audience.

Timing

An important part of ensuring the proper reception for your message is timing. Effective communication is timed well. A memo is going to be given different levels of attention depending on whether it hits someone's desk on Monday morning or on Friday afternoon. A meeting on the Friday before a holiday weekend will be given a different level of attention than if it is postponed until Monday afternoon.

You also need to consider the context of the message. If massive layoffs were announced Monday, Tuesday may not be the best time proudly to proclaim record new earnings. A company received a lot of bad press when, on national "Take Your Daughter to Work Day" in 1995, it informed a man in front of his daughter that he was being let go. An executive who got up to say a few words at a company's holiday party in December became a legend by spending ten minutes very inappropriately talking about the austerity and belt tightening that had to occur in the new year.

Regulating

Regulating the amount of information received by the people who report to you is a useful technique for reducing overload. It is also, unfortunately, dangerous to assume that you know what they need to know! It is possible to take on the role of filter for your group, but it is also time-consuming and subjective. Some managers choose to have their assistants filter their mail, separating the junk mail from the important mail, for example. The danger here is obvious: What is junk to your assistant may not be junk to you.

Trying to regulate upward communication is probably the most difficult task, since honest upward communication is easiest to squelch inadvertently. It is also critical to the smooth running of an organization. As a manager, you need, first of all, to have a plan for effective upward communication. It does not just happen. You need to use several different modes (surveys, open forums, formal and informal channels) and take action in response to what is communicated. Taking action is the most critical step of all. Many organizations have run into diminishing returns from programs that ask for upward communications (such as employee surveys) because employees believe that nothing happens as a result.

Listening

Thus far we have been talking about how to get your message across more effectively when you have something to say. Effective communication involves understanding what other people are saying, as well, and that means honing your listening skills. Most of us do not spend nearly enough time listening, because we think a lot faster than people talk. When people talk to us, our minds are racing ahead, preparing what we will say next or considering our response. No wonder half of what they say is lost.

Really listening requires a lot of work and may require practice if you are not in the habit of listening. Take the time really to pay attention when someone tells you something. Ask questions to clarify what you understood the person to say. We sometimes forget that accurate communication really does start this simply—with two people conversing. We very seldom take the time to listen accurately. People will be very impressed when you do! When done well, listening goes a long way toward ensuring accurate communication. You may then be able to teach the other person to listen to you with the same level of accuracy.

The Forbidden Snack Bar: Part 2

The new manager in the opening example became very aware of possible miscommunications as a result of this initial misunderstanding. He began to solicit feedback from his staff on his style and his manner of communicating. Just paying attention to communication caused him to improve considerably. Someone pointed out to him, for example, that when he was listening intently to something an employee was telling him, he would get a ferocious scowl on his face. To him, this was an intent look signifying concentration. Many employees misinterpreted it as anger, possibly directed at them.

He expanded the feedback that he asked for, and when he didn't "shoot the messenger," he continued to receive it. His assistant manager pointed out that it was inappropriate, when giving an employee an important task to do, to "jokingly" threaten the person with termination if it wasn't done. "I just want them to know that it is very important to me," he said. "Then that's all you need to say," replied the assistant. Now, when this manager says, "This is very important to me," everyone who works for him gets the message loud and clear.

What Do You Need to Know About Communication?

In your personal communications, keep in mind that there are effective and ineffective ways to get your message across. Managers tend to be somewhat careless in talking to subordinates; after all, you're the boss. But your staff is critical to getting the work of your department or division done. With whom is it more important for you to communicate well? (Yes, it is important to communicate well with your boss, but most of us realize that and craft those communications carefully).

When you are in the subordinate role, what works for you? Think of ways that people have communicated with you; note which of these has been effective or ineffective, and use this as guidelines for your communications. Most of us respond poorly to communication that judges us; we become defensive. Remember to describe what you saw or heard, rather than evaluate it; say, for example, "There were three errors in the report you gave me Monday," rather than "You are careless." We also respond defensively to attempts to control us or to communication that sounds all-knowing. Truly explore your employees' perspectives by taking an inquiring tack. If you already have all the answers, you're in trouble. It is also helpful if you show at least a little empathy for what an employee is feeling as he tries to convey something to you. Appearing detached, apathetic, and uninterested in your employees seems very businesslike to some managers, but it is frustrating to an employee who is angry, upset, or thrilled about something. Last, be careful of any tendencies you have toward communicating in a superior ("I am the boss") fashion. Employees know you are the boss. The more you have to try to prove it, the more they may doubt you. If you use your position to intimidate in any way, open communication will be threatened. This is one of those things that it is very hard to be honest with yourself about, so you may wish to ask a trusted associate how you come across to people.

Manager's Checklist

- [ ] Everything you do communicates something. You cannot not communicate! Pay attention to the messages (verbal and nonverbal) that you are sending.
- [ ] Be aware of the effectiveness of the upward, downward, and horizontal communication processes in your organization.
- [ ] Pay attention to the characteristics of the sender, the message, the medium, the receiver, the feedback, and the climate.
- [ ] Analyze the barriers to effective communication in your organization or department. Remember, barriers result from distortions of various kinds in the communications process and from information overload.
- [ ] Improve the communications in your organizations by spending time on analysis, follow-up, repetition, style, timing, and regulating.
- [ ] Work on your listening skills. Practice really listening to understand.

Suggested Reading

The basic psychological concepts in this book are covered in any introductory psychology textbook. Three recent ones are:

Davis, S., and Palladino, J. *Psychology*. Englewood Cliffs, N.J.: Prentice-Hall, 1995.

Morris, C. *Psychology: An Introduction*. 8th ed. Englewood Cliffs, N.J.: Prentice-Hall, 1993.

Worchel, S., and Shebliske, W. *Psychology: Principles and Applications*, 5th ed. Englewood Cliffs, N.J.: Prentice-Hall, 1995.

Chapter 1

For further information on the Myers-Briggs Type Indicator, see:

Keirsey, D., and Bates, M. *Please Understand Me: Character and Temperament Types*. Del Mar, Calif.: Prometheus Nemesis, 1984.

Kroeger, O., and Thuesen, J. *Type Talk at Work*. New York: Bantam Doubleday Dell, 1992.

Myers-Briggs Type Indicator and MBTI are registered trademarks of Consulting Psychologists Press, Palo Alto,

California. Materials are distributed by the Center for Applications of Psychological Type, Gainesville, Florida.

Chapter 4

A good article with more information on Herzberg's theories is:

Herzberg, F. "One More Time: How Do You Motivate Employees?" *Harvard Business Review* (January–February 1968).

Chapter 5

A valuable self-help book for stress management is:

Adams, J. *Understanding and Managing Stress: A Workbook in Changing Life Styles.* San Diego: Pfeiffer and Company, 1980.

Chapter 6

The research referred to in the section on intelligence includes:

Gardner, H. *Multiple Intelligences: The Theory in Practice.* New York: Basic Books, 1993.

Goleman, D. *Emotional Intelligence.* New York: Bantam Doubleday Dell, 1995.

MacLean, P. *The Triune Brain in Evolution.* New York: Plenum, 1990.

Salovey, P., and Mayer, J. "Emotional Intelligence." *Imagination, Cognition and Personality* 9, 1990, pp. 185–211.

Sternberg, R. *Beyond I.Q.* New York: Cambridge University Press, 1985.

Chapters 7 and 8

An introductory social psychology text will provide background on the concepts discussed in these chapters. A recent one is:

Baron, R. *Social Psychology,* 7th ed. Newton, Mass.: Allyn and Bacon, 1994.

For more on groupthink, see:

Janus, I. *Victims of Groupthink.* New York: Houghton Mifflin Company, 1972.

The idea of phased development in groups originated with:

Tuckman, B. "Developmental Sequences in Small Groups." *Psychological Bulletin* 63, 1965, pp. 384–399.

Chapter 9

An academic, research-based book on these topics is:

Pace, R., and Faules, D. *Organizational Communication,* 3rd ed. Englewood Cliffs, New Jersey: Prentice-Hall, 1994.

Index